JACK LONDON

THE CHELSEA HOUSE LIBRARY OF BIOGRAPHY

JACK LONDON

ALAN SCHROEDER

Chelsea House Publishers

New York • Philadelphia

CHELSEA HOUSE PUBLISHERS

Editor-in-Chief   Remmel Nunn
Managing Editor   Karyn Gullen Browne
Copy Chief   Mark Rifkin
Picture Editor   Adrian Allen
Art Director   Maria Epes
Assistant Art Director   Noreen Romano
Manufacturing Manager   Gerald Levine
Systems Manager   Lindsey Ottman
Production Manager   Joseph Romano
Production Coordinator   Marie Claire Cebrián

The Chelsea House Library of Biography
Senior Editor   Kathy Kuhtz

Staff for ***JACK LONDON***
Associate Editor   Scott Prentzas
Copy Editor   Benson D. Simmonds
Editorial Assistant   Tamar Levovitz
Picture Researcher   Joan Beard
Designer   Basia Niemczyc
Cover Illustration   Jim Phalen

3   5   7   9   8   6   4

Library of Congress Cataloging-in-Publication Data

Schroeder, Alan.
Jack London/Alan Schroeder
p. cm.—(Chelsea House library of biography)
Includes bibliographical references and index.
Summary: A biography of the renowned American author focusing on his short, turbulent life and the many adventures that are reflected in his novels and stories.
ISBN   0-7910-1623-4
        0-7910-1630-7 (pbk.)

1. London, Jack, 1876–1916—Biography—Juvenile literature. 2. Authors, American—20th century—Biography—Juvenile literature. [1. London, Jack, 1876–1916. 2. Authors, American.] I. Title. II. Series.

PS3523.046Z874 1991
818'.5209—dc20

91-10282
CIP
AC

Contents

THE CHELSEA HOUSE LIBRARY OF BIOGRAPHY

Other titles in the series are forthcoming.

Introduction

Learning from Biographies

Vito Perrone

The oldest narratives that exist are biographical. Most of what we know, for example, about the Pharaohs of ancient Egypt, the builders of Babylon, the philosophers of Greece, the rulers of Rome, the many biblical and religious leaders who provide the base for contemporary spiritual beliefs, has come to us through biographies—the stories of their lives. Although an oral tradition was long the mainstay of historically important biographical accounts, the oral stories making up this tradition became by the 1st century A.D. central elements of a growing written literature.

In the 1st century A.D., biography assumed a more formal quality through the work of such writers as Plutarch, who left us more than 500 biographies of political and intellectual leaders of Rome and Greece. The tradition of focusing on great personages lasted well into the 20th century, and it is seen as an important means of understanding the history of various times and places. We learn much, for example, from Plutarch's writing about the collapse of the Greek city-states and about the struggles in Rome over the justice and the constitutionality of a world empire. We also gain considerable understanding of the definitions of morality and civil virtue and how various common men and women lived out their daily existence.

Not surprisingly, the earliest American writing, beginning in the 17th century, was heavily biographical. Those Europeans who came to America were dedicated to recording their experience, especially the struggles they faced in building what they determined to be a new culture. John Norton's *Life and Death of John Cotton*, printed in 1630, typifies these early works. Later biographers often tackled more ambitious projects. Cotton Mather's *Magnalia Christi Americana*, published in 1702, accounted for the lives of more than 70 ministers and political leaders. In addition, a biographical literature around the theme of Indian captivity had considerable popularity. Soon after the American Revolution and the organization of the United States of America, Americans were treated to a large outpouring of biographies about such figures as Benjamin Franklin, George Washington, Thomas Jefferson, and Aaron Burr, among others. These particular works served to build a strong sense of national identity.

Among the diverse forms of historical literature, biographies have been over many centuries the most popular. And in recent years interest in biography has grown even greater, as biography has gone beyond prominent government figures, military leaders, giants of business, industry, literature, and the arts. Today we are treated increasingly to biographies of more common people who have inspired others by their particular acts of courage, by their positions on important social and political issues, or by their dedicated lives as teachers, town physicians, mothers, and fathers. Through this broader biographical literature, much of which is featured in the CHELSEA HOUSE LIBRARY OF BIOGRAPHY, our historical understandings can be enriched greatly.

What makes biography so compelling? Most important, biography is a human story. In this regard, it makes of history something personal, a narrative with which we can make an intimate connection. Biographers typically ask us as readers to accompany them on a journey through the life of another person, to see some part of the world through another's eyes. We can, as a result, come to understand what it is like to live the life of a slave, a farmer, a textile worker, an engineer, a poet, a president—in a sense, to walk in another's shoes. Such experience can be personally invaluable. We cannot ask for a better entry into historical studies.

Although our personal lives are likely not as full as those we are reading about, there will be in most biographical accounts many common experiences. As with the principal character of any biography, we are also faced with numerous decisions, large and small. In the midst of living our lives we are not usually able to easily comprehend the significance of our daily decisions or grasp easily their many possible consequences, but we can gain important insights into them by seeing the decisions made by others play themselves out. We can learn from others.

Because biography is a personal story, it is almost always full of surprises. So often, the personal lives of individuals we come across historically are out of view, their public personas masking who they are. It is through biography that we gain access to their private lives, to the acts that define who they are and what they truly care about. We see their struggles within the possibilities and limitations of life, gaining insight into their beliefs, the ways they survived hardships, what motivated them, and what discouraged them. In the process we can come to understand better our own struggles.

As you read this biography, try to place yourself within the subject's world. See the events as that person sees them. Try to understand why the individual made particular decisions and not others. Ask yourself if you would have chosen differently. What are the values or beliefs that guide the subject's actions? How are those values or beliefs similar to yours? How are they different from yours? Above all, remember: You are engaging in an important historical inquiry as you read a biography, but you are also reading a literature that raises important personal questions for you to consider.

Japanese military officials examine Jack London's credentials. London, one of America's most popular writers, went to Japan in 1904 to cover the Russo-Japanese War for the San Francisco Examiner.

1

"It's Not War Correspondence at All"

BY NEW YEAR'S DAY, 1904, the American writer Jack London was aware that political storm clouds were swirling over Japan and Russia. For years, the two countries had been squabbling over each other's economic interests in Korea and Manchuria (a region in northeast China). Despite lengthy negotiations in the fall of 1903, Japan could not persuade Russia to withdraw its troops from Manchuria. Now, with the dawning of the new year, war seemed likely.

Like most people, Jack London was opposed to the idea of armed conflict. But he also realized that if Japan fired on Russia, it would be the biggest news story of the year. American correspondents would be well paid to cover the conflict, and at the moment, London was desperately in need of money: He had only $20.02 in the bank. He was relieved, therefore, when five different news syndicates asked him to cover the fighting.

Though he was only 27 years old, Jack London was considered one of America's most promising young authors. He had already written eight books, among them *The Son of the Wolf*, a strong collection of short stories, and *The People of the Abyss*, a powerful study of the slums of London. His most famous work, however, was *The Call of the Wild*, a gripping adventure story that had catapulted him to the forefront of American literature. Published in the summer of 1903, it was a runaway success, selling 10,000 copies its very first day.

London's name was well known throughout the United States, and with war looming in the Orient, the powerful news syndicates were eager to secure him as a correspondent. "Could have gone for *Harper's*, *Collier's* and N.Y. *Herald*," London later wrote, "but Hearst made the best offer."

On January 7, 1904, London left San Francisco for Yokohama, Japan, on the SS *Siberia*. Unfortunately, the trip got off to a bad start. First, London came down with influenza; then, while roughhousing on deck with the other correspondents, he tripped and sprained his left ankle. "For sixty-five sweaty hours I lay on my back," London wrote in disgust. Years before, in another accident, he had damaged his right ankle, and this new injury nearly crippled him. By the time he arrived in Yokohama, he was barely able to walk.

The correspondents were immediately taken by train to the capital city of Tokyo, where they were lavishly entertained by officials of the Japanese government. War had not yet been declared, and the foreign journalists were only too happy to spend their time attending banquets and visiting picturesque temples. Jack London, however, had not come to Japan to play tourist. Discreetly, he began to make inquiries and was shocked to learn that the Japanese government had no intention of letting the correspondents go anywhere near the fighting.

At this point, London decided to take matters into his own hands. Without telling anyone, he left Tokyo by train, arriving in the southern city of Nagasaki a few days later.

East Asia during the Russo-Japanese War.

His plan was to take a boat across the strait to Korea and from there travel north to Manchuria, where he assumed the fighting would take place. If all went well, he would arrive at the Manchurian battlefront while the other correspondents were still being entertained in Tokyo. It was a brash move, against all government restrictions, but London was determined to get his story.

In the port city of Moji, not far from Nagasaki, London located a steamer bound for Korea. After buying his ticket, he was told that the boat would not begin boarding for another hour. To pass the time, he roamed the streets, taking photographs of the Japanese people. Almost immediately, he was arrested by the police and thrown into jail.

Moji, he later learned, was a military town, and the police suspected London of being a Russian spy. He was questioned and requestioned; his camera was temporarily confiscated. By the time he was released a day later, he had missed his Korea-bound steamer.

At this point, London began to worry. War was about to be declared, and here he was, still in Japan, several hundred miles from the Manchurian border. He was able to book passage on the *Keigo Maru*, but two days before the vessel was to sail, it was confiscated by the Japanese government to transport soldiers. Fortunately, London managed to catch another steamer crossing the strait, but in his wild dash to get aboard, one of his trunks fell into the water.

Upon reaching Korea, London boarded yet another vessel that was supposed to take him north to the port city of Chemulpo (present-day Inchon). But again, maddeningly, the boat was confiscated by the government, and the pas-

Defying the Japanese government's restrictions on war correspondents, London chartered this junk in Mokpo, Korea. He survived a dangerous winter voyage on the Yellow Sea in a valiant attempt to reach the battlefront in Manchuria.

sengers were forced to disembark at Mokpo, a village on the southern tip of the Korean peninsula.

By now, London was nearly frantic. He had no more time to waste, and thinking quickly, he chartered a small boat, with the intention of sailing across the Yellow Sea, then up the coast of Korea until he reached Chemulpo.

It was a simple, but dangerous, plan. The February winds were blowing at gale force, and within hours London had lost his mast and rudder, making it almost impossible to steer the native junk as it plunged haphazardly through the choppy water. At night, the temperature dropped to 14 degrees below zero, and to keep warm London burned a small charcoal brazier on deck. The waves off the Korean coast were 20 feet high, and on numerous occasions, London came perilously close to losing his life. "The wildest and most gorgeous thing ever!" he wrote, colorfully describing what must have been a difficult and miserable voyage.

Another correspondent, an Englishman named Robert Dunn, had also managed, through luck and perseverance, to reach the western coast of Korea. By coincidence, he was in Chemulpo when London arrived at the port. Dunn hardly recognized his exhausted colleague: "[London] was a physical wreck. His ears were frozen; his fingers were frozen; his feet were frozen. He said that he didn't mind his condition so long as he got to the front."

Wasting no time, London outfitted a pack train and set out across the frozen rice fields, making his way north toward the Manchurian border. For the next several weeks, he shared his meals with peasants, interviewed soldiers, and carefully analyzed the strength of the Japanese army. Regularly, he sent out dispatches and photographs, which were prominently featured in the *San Francisco Examiner*.

The other correspondents, meanwhile, were still being entertained in Tokyo. When they heard that London had nearly reached the Manchurian front, they were furious. Why, they demanded, was London the only writer being

Fellow war correspondent Robert Dunn (left) joins London in a lighthearted protest against the Grand Hotel in Seoul, Korea.

allowed to cover the war? Several of the journalists complained to the Japanese government, whose officials saw to it that London was arrested and recalled to Seoul.

For the next three months, Jack London and his colleagues were kept far behind the lines, allowed to see almost nothing of the Russo-Japanese conflict. As the weeks passed, London became increasingly frustrated by his lame-duck position. "Perfect rot I am turning out," he complained bitterly. "It's not war correspondence at all."

Finally, he wrote to the Hearst press, asking permission to report the war from the Russian side. Before he received a reply, however, an incident occurred that brought his stay in the Orient to an abrupt end.

Each of the correspondents had two or three Japanese servants, and London suspected one of these servants, a groom, of being a thief. London quarreled with the man, knocking him to the ground. The Japanese military police chose to interpret this as a hostile action. London was promptly arrested, and there was talk among the Japanese high command of a court-martial and possible execution.

According to some accounts, the most influential of the correspondents, Richard Harding Davis, sent a telegram to President Theodore Roosevelt, explaining the seriousness of the situation. Alarmed, Roosevelt quickly wired the Japanese government, demanding London's release.

By this time, London was thoroughly disgusted and ready to go home: "I've wasted five months of my life in this war!" As quickly as he could, he packed his bags and returned to Yokohama, where, in late June, he caught a ship for San Francisco.

London's colleagues must have had mixed feelings about seeing him go. Naturally, they were jealous of his accomplishments in the field, but at the same time, they secretly admired his brashness and his tenacity, his fierce refusal to let anything stand in the way of success. These qualities, by their very nature, were controversial, but without them, London would never have become one of the most celebrated men of his generation.

A fellow correspondent, Robert Dunn, made no attempt to hide his admiration for his young colleague: "I want to say that Jack London is one of the grittiest men it has been my good fortune to meet. He is just as heroic as any of the characters in his novels."

Jack London, age 10, poses with his dog, Rollo. "I never had a boyhood," London would later remark. "I seem to be hunting for that lost boyhood."

2

The Spirit of Revolt

JACK LONDON'S FATHER, William Chaney, was a man who could never stay in one place for very long. For most of his life, Chaney was a wanderer and a schemer. To some, he was a profound thinker; to others, a gentle crackpot who rarely finished anything he started.

Born into a New England farming family, Chaney dreamed of becoming a pirate. He joined the navy instead, only to desert nine months later. Distrustful of other people and prone to arguments, he abandoned one wife after another, one occupation after another. Carpenter, seaman, editor, lawyer, novelist, teacher, lecturer: William Chaney tried his hand at them all.

Only one field managed to hold his interest—astrology. Traveling around the country, Chaney collected books on spiritualism, arranged séances, studied the planets, and, in larger cities, attended astrological meetings. In the late 19th century, it was fashionable for the upper classes to dabble in the occult, and in the early months of 1874, William Chaney was operating a small astrology parlor in San Francisco. By

Moody and self-absorbed, Flora Wellman London often acted with indifference toward her family. Jack usually felt uneasy in her presence.

then, he was living with his fourth wife, Flora Wellman, a short, high-strung woman in her early thirties.

Flora had grown up the youngest child in a wealthy household in Massillon, Ohio. As a toddler, she had been extremely spoiled by her father, Marshall Wellman, a wheat merchant. At an early age, Flora was stricken with typhoid fever, which not only damaged her looks and eyesight but stunted her growth; as an adult, she stood less than five feet high. The fever also left her with fits of melancholia and instability, which would afflict her frequently in the years to come. Before she was 17, Flora ran away from home. A few years later, she arrived in San Francisco, where she gave piano lessons to support herself. In June 1874, she took up residence with William Chaney, and together they operated their astrology parlor on Bush Street.

"Professor" Chaney, as he was called, took his profession very seriously. Astrology, in his opinion, was a science, capable of achieving great advancements for mankind. He believed, for instance, that it was possible for a man and a woman to produce a biologically superior child—all that was necessary was a careful consultation of the stars. Chaney considered the matter nearly foolproof, as scientific as any chemistry experiment. And yet he had no desire to be a father himself. When Flora told him, in the summer of 1875, that she was expecting a child, Chaney panicked. He demanded that she terminate the pregnancy. Flora refused, the two quarreled, and, after a long and bitter argument, Chaney ordered her out of the house. The relationship, he said, was finished.

Now it was Flora's turn to panic. She could not imagine life without Chaney, and she immediately took an overdose of opium. When this failed to do the job, she seized a secondhand pistol, aimed it at her forehead, and fired. Fortunately, the bullet glanced off, leaving her with nothing more than a nasty flesh wound. The *San Francisco Chronicle* had a field day with the story, dwelling on every detail of the "Heartlessness and Domestic Misery" of the Chaney household. A few months later, William Chaney packed his things and departed for the Pacific Northwest, never to return.

After Flora's head wound had been treated, she was taken to the home of an acquaintance, where she spent many weary months in bed, struggling to regain her mental stability. During this time, she must have discovered a reason for living; in any event, she made no further attempt at suicide, and, six months later, on January 12, 1876, she gave birth to a son, whom she named John Griffith Chaney. Too sickly to nurse the child, Flora sent the boy to live with Virginia Prentiss, a black woman who had recently lost her own baby and was willing to nurse Flora's. It was an ideal arrangement, and, for the next nine months, "Aunt Jennie" showered the boy with love and attention, raising him like her own son.

Flora, meanwhile, attempted to rebuild her life. She began giving piano lessons again, and, before the year was out, she had met and married a middle-aged Civil War veteran named John London. A widower, London had recently arrived from the Midwest with his two daughters, Eliza and Ida, whom he had temporarily placed in the Protestant Orphan Asylum. Considering the circumstan-

Jack London's father, William Chaney, was a lifelong drifter. When Flora Wellman informed him that she was pregnant with his child, Chaney ended their relationship and left San Francisco. Years later, Chaney responded to London's letters to him by flatly denying that he was Jack's father.

ces, John's proposal of marriage was entirely practical. Flora, alone and deeply depressed, would benefit from a stable home life, and John needed a helpmate and mother for his two young children. He and Flora were married in September 1876, and shortly thereafter, Flora went to Mrs. Prentiss's to retrieve her son John. Years later, when the boy was about 10, his name was changed to Jack, and it was by this name—Jack London—that he would become known to the world.

Though they shared no physical resemblance, Jack grew up believing that John London was his father. More than 20 years later, having heard rumors about William Chaney, Jack decided to find out the truth for himself. He wrote to the astrologer, who was then residing in Chicago, asking him to explain the lurid story in the *San Francisco Chronicle* that Jack had recently discovered in the public library. Chaney wrote back twice, insisting each time that he could not possibly be Jack's father: "I was impotent at that time," he explained, "the result of hardship, privation & too much brain-work." Of course, Flora could have explained everything to Jack, but her moods were unpredictable, and, to avoid an unpleasant scene, he refrained from discussing the subject with her. As a result, Jack went through life never knowing for sure who his natural father was.

During Jack's early years, John London worked as a door-to-door salesman for the Singer Sewing Machine Company. Unfortunately, his lungs had been damaged during the Civil War, and extended walking tired him. Moreover, he lacked the aggressive personality necessary to become a successful salesman. His income, understandably, was meager, and the family was constantly moving from one house to another. The economics of poverty were harsh: When Jack and his stepsister Eliza caught diphtheria, Flora wondered aloud if it would not be cheaper to bury both bodies in one coffin, if the children should die.

John London, Jack's stepfather, married Flora Wellman in September 1876. Jack grew up believing that London was his biological father.

From the beginning, Flora resisted her duties as wife and mother. Moody and self-absorbed, she was not interested in the family's day-to-day affairs. Like countless others, Flora had come to San Francisco because it had seemed, to her midwestern eyes, a city of unlimited possibilities; instead, she had found only poverty and despair. She became a bitter, scheming woman, and almost always, Jack felt uneasy in her presence.

Unable to make a living as a sewing machine salesman, John moved his family across the San Francisco Bay to the city of Oakland, where he tried his hand at farming. He found that he was able to sell his produce quickly, and, encouraged by this success, he leased a 20-acre farm in Alameda, a few miles to the west. It was here, in Alameda, that Jack first went to school, tagging along with his older stepsister, Eliza. She was quick to notice that Jack always seemed to have a book in his hand. Sitting in class, he loved poring over the illustrations, and, gradually, he began to learn to read.

Unfortunately, it was also in Alameda that Jack had his first encounter with alcohol. He was nearly seven at the time, and the experience left him badly shaken. His stepfather, John, was in the habit of quenching his thirst from a small pail of beer, which Jack obediently carried to him in the field. One day, Jack decided to taste some of the beer himself. One swallow led to another, and by the time he reached his stepfather, Jack was feeling pleasantly tipsy. Later, under the trees at the edge of the field, he became sick to his stomach.

Sadly, this youthful incident did not steer him away from alcohol, and, years later, Jack's fear of alcoholism would become the subject of one of his most influential books, *John Barleycorn*. "I was aware of deadly nausea," he wrote, remembering that singular day in the field. "My condition was like that of one who had gone through a battle with poison. In truth, I had been poisoned. . . . There was no escaping [John Barleycorn]."

On Jack's seventh birthday, in January 1883, the family loaded a horse-drawn wagon and moved yet again, this time across the bay to a San Mateo potato ranch. Flora was optimistic about the move. She believed that by growing the finest potatoes in the Bay Area, she and John could recapture the wealthy life-style she had known during her youth. The only drawback, in her opinion, was the proximity of the immigrant neighbors, many of whom were Italian. Flora was excessively proud of the racial "purity" of her family, and she raised Jack with the belief that dark-eyed, dark-skinned races could not be trusted. In her own words, the average foreigner was "profoundly treacherous," a crafty devil eager to "stab you in the back." Jack was never able to shake his mother's racist attitude, and, reading his works today, it is one of his most unattractive qualities. (It should be noted, however, that racial prejudice was by no means uncommon during the late 19th century. The majority of Caucasians in the United States would not have been offended by Jack's racial beliefs.)

Happily, the cool, foggy climate of San Mateo proved ideal for potato raising. Though Jack disliked the drudgery of field work, he looked forward to the periodic wagon trips to San Francisco to sell the harvest. His stepfather usually stopped at a roadside bar along the way, and years later Jack carried with him rich memories of the potbellied stoves, the intimate laughter, the heavy mugs of beer, and, most fantastically, the "delicious dainties" spread out, free of charge, at one end of the bar: pungent sausages, cheeses, tins of sardines, crackers, and thick bologna sandwiches. On one occasion, Jack recalled, the bartender "mixed me a sweet temperance drink of syrup and soda water. My father did not pay for it. It was the barkeeper's treat, and he became my ideal of a good, kind man."

Like most children, Jack was highly impressionable. After two or three such visits, he came to the conclusion that saloons were warm, friendly places—always open, always inviting. "Glass in hand! . . ." he later wrote with a

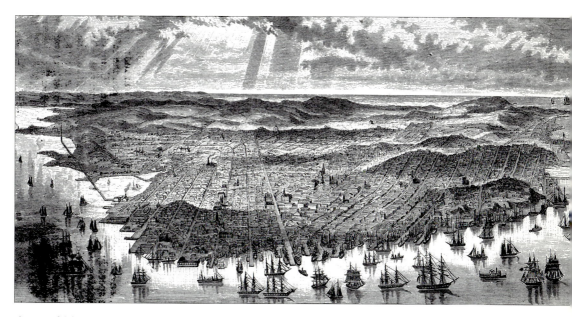

tinge of bitterness. "It is a habit of mind to which I have been trained all my life."

By the time Jack was eight, Flora had grown tired of the potato-raising business. She was an impatient person, always convinced that the grass was greener elsewhere. As soon as John had saved enough money, the family moved yet again, this time settling on a large farm in Livermore, a hot agricultural town not far from Oakland. For once, Jack was able to attend a decent school, and John's good-sized orchard provided enough food for the entire family. The 87-acre farm, however, was isolated, and Jack spent most of his time alone, reading. Books, understandably, became his dearest companions, and he dreamed of the day when he could build himself a spacious home, with one entire room set aside for cherished volumes.

By now, 16-year-old Eliza was performing most of the household chores, including the cooking and the washing. The responsibility of raising Jack also fell onto her shoulders. One day, when Jack cut his forehead while playing, Eliza calmly treated the wound by smearing it with a mixture of cobwebs and tar. The homemade remedy was

A bird's-eye view of San Francisco in 1875, one year before Jack London's birth. During Jack's childhood, the London family moved frequently throughout the San Francisco Bay Area in a quest to attain the level of wealth and success that Flora coveted.

effective: The resulting scar is not visible in any photographs. Jack never forgot his stepsister's kindness, and in the years to come, he would repay her many times over.

Flora, meanwhile, continued to pursue her interest in spiritualism. She held regular séances, and Jack vividly remembered one occasion when the table at which they were sitting apparently lifted itself into the air. Flora was also in the habit of consulting the departed spirits on financial matters. More often than not, the spirits encouraged her to invest in Chinese lottery tickets. Jack himself never adopted his mother's fascination for the occult, though one of his last books, *The Star Rover*, dealt extensively with the themes of reincarnation and soul travel.

Everything that year seemed to be going well. The crops were healthy, the henhouses were flourishing, and Flora had enough pocket money to treat Jack to a pair of store-bought underwear, a luxury. Then, unexpectedly, disaster struck. An epidemic killed most of the chickens, and John, unable to pay the bank, lost the house. It was also at this time that Eliza married a Civil War veteran named James Shepard and moved away.

Once again, the potato wagon was loaded up, and, discouraged, the family moved back to Oakland. John's great dream of independence seemed permanently shattered. He became a night watchman, and, gradually, the family slipped back into a life of near poverty. Flora, using what little money they had, set up a boardinghouse for women, but this, too, was unsuccessful. Failure haunted the family's every step.

At the age of ten, Jack was enrolled at the Garfield School, but, quite soon, he discovered another world that seemed far richer than that of any classroom, a world that contained all knowledge, all truth: the Oakland Public Library. There, sitting on the high shelves, were books on every subject imaginable, and Jack began checking out as many as he could. "I read everything . . ." he remembered. "I read mornings, afternoons, and nights. I read in bed, I read at table, I read as I walked to and from school, and I read at recess while the other boys were playing." The library, he sensed, was not only a grand, silent place, filled with knowledge, but, in some odd way, it also contained the key to success. Years later, in his novel *Martin Eden*, Jack described the sense of wonder and fear that he must have felt walking through the tall stacks of the cool, cavernous library:

> [Martin] had never dreamed that the fund of human knowledge bulked so big. He was frightened. How could his brain ever master it all? Later, he remembered that there were other men, many men, who had mastered it; and he breathed a great oath, passionately, under his breath, swearing that his brain could do what theirs had done.

Reading became the most important part of Jack's life. It offered him an escape from the poverty around him; his day-to-day world seemed more exciting, more meaningful, whenever he was absorbed in the pages of a novel. Jack was especially fond of sea stories. Reading Herman Melville's *Typee* and *White-Jacket*, he could feel the choppiness of the water, smell the sea spray in his nostrils. Fortunately, Oakland was a waterfront city, and Jack could often be found down at the wharf, watching the schooners and the fishing boats as they headed out toward the Golden Gate Strait. Like many boys, Jack dreamed of sailing the seven seas, a cutlass between his teeth. But, at the age of 10, he was still too young to sign on as a ship's mate.

In any event, his presence was needed at home. As John London's health began to fail, it became necessary for Jack to accept odd jobs to supplement the family income. He was a strong, silent child, very serious for his age. After school, he delivered newspapers and, on Saturdays, helped the iceman make the rounds. He cut lawns, trimmed hedges, and set up pins in a bowling alley. Flora took most

In the late 19th century, child laborers operate a spinning machine in a New England textile mill. Jack, like many children of his generation, began working at a young age to help support his family financially.

of his earnings—once a week, she fished in her apron pocket and handed Jack a dime, which he could spend however he wished.

Sometimes he bought a balcony seat at the Tivoli Theater, but just as often, he would buy a thick slab of saltwater taffy and visit one of Oakland's saloons. He never drank; he simply wanted to feel that he was part of something exciting. "In the saloons," he remembered, "life

was different. Men talked with great voices, laughed great laughs. . . . Here life was always very live, and, sometimes, even lurid, when blows were struck, and blood was shed, and big policemen came shouldering in. . . . [E]ven the sots, stupefied, sprawling across the tables or in the sawdust, were objects of mystery and wonder."

With a heavy slingshot wedged in his back pocket, Jack spent many afternoons in the reedy marshes of San Leandro Bay, hunting for ducks and mud hens. He also roamed the hills behind Lake Merritt, hoping to snare a wildcat. On one thrilling occasion, he was even allowed aboard the sloop *Idler*, which was rumored to be engaged in opium smuggling. Below deck, the sailors were sharing drinks, and for hours, Jack listened to fantastic stories of the sea—of courage, and near death, and fierce Arctic winds that smashed whaleboats like toothpicks. It was a glorious, drunken afternoon, with singing and laughter and sloppy vows of eternal friendship. Jack boasted of his ability to steer a small boat, and the sailors seemed properly impressed. And all the while, drinks were being poured, one after the other, and Jack, to his amazement, was holding his own with these hardened sailors with stomachs of iron.

"I could carry my drink," he wrote in *John Barleycorn*. "I was a man. . . . It was [that afternoon] that I discovered what a good stomach and a strong head I had for drink—a bit of knowledge that was to be a source of pride in succeeding years, and that ultimately I [came] to consider a great affliction."

These adventurous afternoons would soon come to an end, however. At the age of 14, Jack graduated from the Cole Grammar School in West Oakland. Lacking a suit, and unable to afford one, he was forced to skip his graduation ceremony. High school was out of the question— higher education, Flora felt, was a luxury the family could hardly afford. Instead, Jack was sent to work at a local cannery. There he had his first exposure to hard labor. It was an experience he never forgot.

The job was simple, and nightmarish. Hour after hour, Jack stood in front of a machine, manually squeezing pickles into glass jars. Looking around, he was horrified at what he saw. Young men and old men stood side by side, bleary-eyed, their spirits crushed after years of toil; women of 19 and 20 were already hunched over, despair creasing their faces. The cannery whistle blew at seven in the morning, and the workers were allowed to leave at six o'clock in the evening. It was not uncommon, however, to work a 15- or 18-hour day, and, on one occasion, Jack worked for 36 hours straight, cramming a sandwich into his mouth to keep up his strength. The pay was only 10 cents an hour, and Jack quickly saw what the others apparently did not: that if he continued to work at the cannery, the hard work would eventually ruin his body. Nobody could be worked like a horse day in and day out, year in and year out.

Every night, Jack fell into bed, exhausted. He was too tired to read, almost too tired to eat. He dreamed vaguely of buying a boat, but, at 10 cents an hour, this seemed impossible. The more Jack thought about his job, the greater his anguish. He knew that after a few years, he would become nothing more than a work beast, an animal with no hope, no ambition, and no future. It was a terrifying thought, and yet there seemed to be no alternative. Ten cents an hour . . . 10 cents an hour: The hopelessness of it all tortured him.

Finally, at the age of 15, Jack was driven to an act of desperation. For several years, he had heard about the daring oyster pirates who roamed the San Francisco Bay, stealing by night from the private oyster beds and selling their "catch" the next morning at the wharf for a handsome profit. Pirating was illegal, of course, but to Jack it had always sounded like a thrilling adventure, much more interesting than working in a cannery. When he heard, that summer, that a local seaman was selling his boat, the *Razzle Dazzle*, Jack resolved not to let the opportunity pass. He borrowed $300 from his old wet nurse, Aunt Jennie, and, hurrying down to Johnny Heinold's First and Last Chance Saloon, he bought the secondhand sloop from French Frank, sealing the bargain over a bottle of whiskey.

It was on this day, Jack remembered, that he had his first taste "of the spirit of revolt, of adventure, of romance, of the things forbidden and done defiantly and grandly. And I knew that on the morrow I would not go back to my machine at the cannery. To-morrow I would be an oyster pirate, as free a freebooter as the century and the waters of San Francisco Bay would permit."

London reminisces with French Frank, a chum from his oyster pirate days. London bought a secondhand sloop, the Razzle Dazzle, *from French Frank in 1891, launching his daring, albeit short, career as an oyster pirate.*

London strikes a pensive pose for his high school portrait. He enrolled in Oakland High School in 1895, but he dropped out to prepare for the University of California's entrance exam.

3

Manhood's Spurs

CALIFORNIA OYSTERS were not as tasty as eastern oysters, but they fetched a high price nonetheless, and the beds were closely guarded by their owners. It was a serious crime to steal oysters in the San Francisco Bay, but Jack was willing to take the risk. Aunt Jennie warned him that he might end up going to prison, but Jack was not bothered by this possibility. The *Razzle Dazzle* was his, and that was all that mattered. As soon as he could comfortably steer the sloop and hoist its sails, he launched himself into the fine and dangerous profession of oyster piracy.

Two things were required to be a successful pirate: speed and courage. Jack had an abundance of both. Within a few weeks, he was bringing in oyster loads as large as any pirate's on the bay. His reputation, he remembered, "became immediately excellent. I was looked upon as a good fellow, as well as no coward." Later, when Jack became an author, he would romanticize this period in such books as *John Barleycorn* and *The Cruise of the Dazzler*, but, in truth, pirating was dirty, dangerous work, and more than one daring "wharf rat" ended up behind bars in San Quentin.

After dark, using only a running light for illumination, Jack would select an oyster bed and quietly drop his anchor. Then, changing to a flat-bottomed skiff, he would make his way up the soft mud flats and, working quickly, load his sloop with as many oysters as possible. All the while, he remained on the lookout not only for armed watchmen but for the vigilant California Fish Patrol, whose deputies cruised the bay hoping to catch the pirates red-handed. If danger was too close—or if the beds had already been picked over by another pirate—Jack was not above raiding the nets of private fishermen, filling the *Razzle Dazzle* with trout and good-sized sturgeon. The next morning, if all had gone well, Jack would have buckets of fresh seafood to sell to the merchants at the crowded Oakland wharf.

Stealing may have been disagreeable to Jack's conscience, but the money he made from oyster pirating was irresistible. For one night's work, he pocketed no less than $25; working overtime in the cannery, he might have earned this much in 3 weeks. He was also meeting some of the liveliest characters in all of California: "Big" George, Clam, Spider Healy, Stew Kennedy, and, of course, Mamie, the "Queen of the Pirates." Though he was only 15, Jack was immediately accepted into this rough-and-tumble crowd, and within a few months, his skill, speed, and recklessness had earned him the title of "Prince of the Oyster Pirates," an honor he cherished for years.

"And so I won my manhood's spurs," Jack proudly wrote, but these spurs could sometimes be disagreeable, as he quickly learned at the bar of Heinold's First and Last Chance Saloon. Every pirate, he noticed, drank large quantities of whiskey and beer. In those days, in that environment, it was part of being a man, and Jack wanted desperately to be a man. He did not care for the taste of whiskey, but he was not about to have Clam or Nicky the

Greek call him a sissy, and, when the old sailors bellied up to the bar, Jack was right there, ready to match them drink for drink. Even when he began to stagger and had to grip the bar for support, he would continue ordering. To refuse a drink with a fellow pirate would have been antisocial, out of the question. Getting drunk with good friends, as Jack saw it, was "a social duty and a manhood rite."

But always, after a rip-roaring night of whiskey and red wine, he suffered the inevitable hangover, the vomiting, and, worst of all, a growing awareness that his behavior was strangely suicidal. For every "mad, magnificent" hour of drunkenness, there was a corresponding low, a fierce depression that Jack was finding harder and harder to shake. One evening, after drinking heavily, he stumbled off a boat, and, swiftly, the current began to carry him away. At first, he was amused by this misadventure, and, bobbing along, he let the tide have its way with him. The bracing water, he remembered, felt "delicious" against his hot, tingling skin.

Then, quite suddenly, the thought of suicide entered Jack's head. The idea seemed attractive, "a splendid culmination," he later wrote, "a perfect rounding off of my short but exciting career. . . . I decided that this was all, that I had seen all, lived all, been all . . . and that now was the time to cease." Only at the last moment did Jack change his mind and begin paddling for his life. Fortunately, a fisherman was nearby, and, hearing Jack's shouts, he pulled the boy to safety.

Years later, in his book *John Barleycorn*, Jack described that night in vivid detail. Alcoholism, he concluded, was a long and dangerous "path that leads down into the grave." His suicide attempt, he knew, was not the act of a rational person; it was a "monstrous, incredible trick" that alcohol had played upon him. And yet it took another disastrous night of drinking to convince Jack that he was courting death. While carousing with friends, he was guzzling whiskey when he was stricken with the terrible sensation that

At age 17, London signed up as an able-bodied seaman on the Sophia Sutherland, *which set sail for Japan and the Bering Sea to hunt seals.*

he was drowning. Panicked, he smashed a window and began gulping great quantities of air into his lungs, but this did not prevent him from falling into a 17-hour coma. "I often think it is the nearest to death I have ever been," Jack admitted sadly.

It was this experience, more than any other, that forced him to moderate his drinking. After reviving from his alcohol-induced coma, Jack decided that his life-style was entirely too reckless: "It made toward death too quickly to suit my youth and vitality." Courageously, he quit the profession of oyster piracy and, in short order, got a job with the California Fish Patrol, cruising the waters of the North Bay for Greek and Chinese fishermen using illegal nets. But again, the temptation of John Barleycorn was too near. Jack saw that the crewmen of the fish patrol enjoyed their liquor just as much as the oyster pirates. Dismayed, he began looking for a new profession.

For some months, the urge to travel had been tickling Jack's fancy. He was eager for new sights and new adventures. Above all, he wanted to taste the raw, salty life the sailors bragged about in the Oakland saloons. One day, he happened to meet a harpooner named Pete Holt, who told him vivid stories of seal hunting in the frigid Arctic. Jack listened, fascinated, and, sensing his enthusiasm, Holt encouraged him to sign on as an able-bodied seaman on the *Sophia Sutherland*, a three-masted schooner preparing to sail from the Bay Area. Jack needed no prompting. He immediately signed the necessary papers, and, two weeks after his 17th birthday, in January of 1893, he sailed through the Golden Gate, bound for the coast of Japan.

Jack quickly adapted to life aboard the 150-ton schooner. Just as he had done with the oyster pirates, he listened and learned, and within a matter of weeks was able to tie any variety of knot, steer by compass, and—crucially—hold his own with the older, more experienced seamen. These hardened sailors wanted nothing more than to see the landlubber fail, and Jack's stamina was constantly being tested. Occasionally, he was provoked into a fight, but his agility and quick fists earned him the grudging respect of his opponents. Even "Red John," the ship's bully, kept his distance after a nasty struggle in which Jack nearly gouged out the Swede's eyes. From that day forward, the landlubber was accepted as an equal.

The Pacific crossing lasted 51 days, and Jack's happiest hours were spent alone in his bunk, reading. Books continued to be his closest companions, and, before leaving for Japan, he had crammed his seabags with dozens of volumes. There could not have been many opportunities for quiet reading, however. The *Sophia Sutherland* was a busy sealing schooner, and Jack was expected to pull his own weight. He made it known that he was skilled at handling a boat on the open water, and, before long, Jack was given his chance at the wheel, guiding the *Sophia* through a fierce sea storm. The challenge was exhilarating: "With my own hands I . . . guided a hundred tons of wood and iron through a few million tons of wind and waves. . . . Every fibre of me is thrilling with it. It is very natural. . . . It is success."

After docking at the Bonin Islands for water and repairs, the *Sophia* set sail again, this time heading for the sunless north. For the next three months, she cruised the fog-enshrouded waters off the coast of Japan, hunting for seals. This was the most strenuous, most competitive part of the voyage. It was also, in Jack's opinion, the most nauseating. Week after week, he was forced to drag the squirming seals aboard, where they were struck with clubs and then stripped of their skins. The deck was always slippery with blood and fat; the acrid intestinal odor was revolting. While the skins were being salted, the carcasses were heaved back into the sea, where they were consumed by hungry sharks. The whole brutal process of killing depressed Jack, and when the *Sophia* eventually returned to San Francisco after seven months at sea, he had no desire to sign on for a second voyage.

In Oakland, Jack was again faced with the need for immediate employment. He shuddered at the thought of returning to the cannery, certain that there had to be a better way to make a living. Most of all, he wanted a job that would give him dignity, a measure of self-respect, but in the fall of 1893, jobs of any kind were hard to come by. During Jack's absence, a nationwide depression had sent finances reeling. The dollar was devalued, banks were folding almost daily, and agricultural output was dwindling. To make matters worse, the growing use of machinery in factories was putting many people out of work. Competition for jobs was fierce, and, to Jack's disappointment, the only work he could find was in a jute mill—10 hours a day, 10 cents an hour, the same salary he had been making at the cannery. Again, Jack despised the menial work, which involved nothing more interesting than winding jute twine around a spinning bobbin, hour after hour. His spirits quickly sank in this dingy factory environment.

His mother, meanwhile, continued to dream of wealth. One day, while scanning the newspaper, Flora spotted a writing contest that was open to anyone under the age of

22; the prize for the best piece of descriptive writing was $25. That evening, when her son returned home from the mill, Flora met him at the door, newspaper in hand. She told him that he had to enter the contest, and quickly, before the deadline passed. Jack was too tired, and discouraged, to consider the matter. He shrugged his shoulders and went to bed.

Flora did not give up so easily. Day after day, she talked about the contest. She reminded Jack of his voyage on the *Sophia Sutherland*; surely he could describe some incident aboard the ship that would make for a good story. At last, to please his mother, Jack agreed to enter the contest, and, for the next three nights, working by the light of an oil lamp, he wrote about the time he had taken the ship's wheel, guiding the *Sophia* through the stormy northern

This 1871 drawing depicts a seal hunt in the Bering Sea. London declined to sign on for a second voyage on the Sophia Sutherland; *the cruelty and stench of the kill had disgusted him.*

During the period of widespread unemployment caused by the depression of 1893, police officers herd a group of vagrants into a state workhouse. Returning from his seven-month adventure on the Sophia Sutherland *in August 1893, London was disappointed that the only work he could find was in a jute mill.*

waters. He handed the finished copy to Flora, who took it across the bay herself to the offices of the *San Francisco Morning Call.* On November 12, 1893, the newspaper announced its first-prize winner: Jack London, for his "Story of a Typhoon Off the Coast of Japan." The article, which was published in the *Call,* had been edited by the judges, but even today it remains a vivid narrative, filled with the raw, tense qualities that would characterize so much of London's later writing.

Flora must have sensed her son's literary talent, and it took little encouragement for him to dash off a second story, which was submitted to the *Call* and promptly rejected. The writing contest was over, the editor explained, and the paper could not use any further sea material. London sent the story to other publications, but it was not accepted, and, before he knew it, he had fallen back into the hopeless drudgery of winding jute twine around a spinning bobbin. The only thing that kept him going was the promise of a raise; when this failed to come, he quit in bitterness and began shoveling coal for the Oakland, San Leandro, and Haywards Electric Railway for $30 a month.

The work was backbreaking, but London's supervisor promised him that if he worked hard, he would eventually rise to the top of the company. In the meantime, it was 13 hours a day of sheer hell. When London got home at night, he was too tired to eat, too tired even to undress himself for bed. Only after several weeks was he told the bitter truth: He had been hired to do the work of two men, thereby saving the company $50 a month. London felt deeply betrayed; there was something wrong with capitalism, he believed, when a person could not earn an honest day's pay for an honest day's work. He quit his job, went home, and slept for 24 hours straight. Never again, he swore, would he allow himself to be treated like a work beast.

As the depression of 1893–97 worsened, scores of Americans were finding themselves thrown out of work. Feelings of desperation and bitterness were sweeping the nation. Thousands of people, like London, believed that the system was wrong, that it was unfair for employees to be paid minimal wages while the bosses rode in expensive carriages and sent their children to private schools. In several states, armies began to form, armies made up of the unemployed, the discouraged, and the angry. In the spring of 1894, these various detachments set off for Washington, D.C., where, it was hoped, the government would listen to their complaints. The Industrial Army, as it was sometimes called, caught the popular imagination, and, after talking it over with Flora, London decided to join the local regiment, which had just left Oakland for Sacramento.

Trying to catch up, London rode the rails illegally, clinging to the platform boards beneath the trains. "Riding the blinds" was extremely dangerous, and, on one occasion, a spark from the engine ignited London's clothing; frantically, he tore off his coat, which was immediately sucked into the clattering wheels.

After 10 nerve-racking days, London joined a rear detachment of the army at the summit of the Rocky Mountains. It was snowing, and, shivering badly, London squeezed his way into the crowded refrigerator car that was taking the regiment east. Before he had a chance to sit down, he was seized by the shoulders and tossed to the other side of the boxcar; there, a second man did exactly the same, throwing him into the arms of a third. Like a rag doll, London was tossed back and forth until he reached the far end of the car. This strange ritual was the army's way of welcoming him to the regiment.

Riding east, the men kept themselves warm by telling jokes and sipping from thin flasks of whiskey. There was a feeling of camaraderie in the air, a sense of purpose that many had never known before. To pass the hours, they shared stories of unemployment and abominable working conditions; undoubtedly, London described in vivid detail his jobs at the cannery, the jute mill, and the railway company. Eighty-six strong, the men felt invincible. They were anxious to get to Washington, where they would stand with their brothers on the steps of the Capitol and demand their rights. Their bravado was contagious, and London was extremely happy. He had $10 in his pocket and good friends at his side. Success seemed inevitable.

A few days later, the train reached Omaha, Nebraska, where a much larger detachment was stationed. London never forgot his first dispiriting sight of the famed Industrial Army. It was two o'clock in the morning, pouring rain, and 1,600 men were crowded together in a local park.

Jacob Coxey's army marches toward Washington, D.C., in 1894. That year, several groups of unemployed workers, including Coxey's army, went to the nation's capital to demand relief legislation. London joined such a contingent from California called Kelly's army.

Fatigue, hunger, and six inches of mud had dampened everyone's spirits. It was nearly impossible to keep a fire lit, and fistfights broke out over the few available blankets. London walked several miles into town for food but came up empty-handed. He spent the night sleeping in a deserted saloon.

The following day, it was still raining, but the army set out anyway, marching east. Public sympathy for the cause was strong, and, in most towns, the citizens donated money and food to keep the army going. This was not enough, however, to keep up the men's morale. The stinging rain was accompanied by hail, making the roads a slippery mess. The midwestern railroads refused to transport the regiment, and, with a shortage of wagons, there was angry talk among the men of seizing a train. Stumbling along the muddy paths, London must have realized he was poorly dressed for the journey. His thin shirt was thoroughly drenched, and his secondhand shoes offered no protection or support. Exhaustion began to set in.

Within a week, London's feet were hopelessly blistered. He began falling behind. Repeatedly, he asked for a new pair of shoes, but the army, he was told, was not sufficiently equipped to provide clothing to its men. Discouraged, London hobbled along, listening to the complaints of the men around him. Many, like himself, had begun to question the usefulness of the march. What if the politicians in

Washington refused to listen? What if the citizens withheld food? When it was all over, how would the army get back home? No one knew the answers.

At night, the men would set up camp in an open field, and, stretched out by a bonfire, London would rest his aching feet. After dinner, cigarettes and whiskey were brought out, and the talk would usually turn to politics. Every man, it seemed, wanted to change the government, and it was probably here, under the starry midwestern skies, that London was first introduced to the principles of socialism.

From what he could gather, capitalism was an unjust system because it allowed only a few people to share the wealth while the majority struggled to survive. Socialism, on the other hand, would see to it that the profits were divided more or less equally, thereby offering hope to the average worker. Under socialism, London was told, the working class would no longer be exploited; in fact, the very concept of social rank would eventually be obliterated. The Socialist Labor party was also opposed to the private ownership of major industries, such as railroads and steel factories. It is not difficult to understand London's early attraction to socialism. It sounded not only fair but sensible, and it provided him with the fervor necessary to continue the often grueling march to Washington.

By the time the army left Des Moines, Iowa, London's shoes were reduced to tatters, and for several days he was forced to walk the trail barefoot. The army meals were barely sufficient to keep up his strength, and on many occasions he abandoned the ranks and wandered door-to-door through the small farming towns, begging for extra food. Eventually, starvation got the better of London. He could march no farther, and, hoping to have greater success on his own, he deserted the army in mid-May. Without a clear plan in mind, he struck out for Chicago, where he roamed the deserted grounds of the World's Columbian Exposition, which had closed a few months earlier. Then, drifting east, he decided to visit Niagara Falls, a move he would bitterly regret. There, the police spotted him as a hobo, and, since vagrancy was a crime, London was arrested, hauled before a judge, and sentenced to 30 days in the Erie County Penitentiary.

Prison was one of the worst, most humiliating experiences of London's life. The first day, he was given a quick shave and haircut. Then, he remembered, he was locked into a cell filled with "degenerates, wrecks, lunatics, addled intelligences, epileptics, monsters . . . a very nightmare of humanity." Violence within the prison was commonplace, and horrifying. Guards thought nothing of hitting a prisoner in the face with a broom handle; rape and battery among the inmates were common. Penitentiary life was brutal and demeaning, and London would never forgive the "system" for sentencing him to a punishment that he felt did not fit the crime.

Years later, he expressed his anger in *The Road*, a vivid collection of essays documenting his tramping experiences. Readers were shocked by its violence, but London was a writer who believed that truth should be held up like a bloody, squirming beast; if it was upsetting to look at, so much the better. Social change, in his opinion, required much more than soft words and passive images. Books had to reflect life itself, bluntly, without compromise.

After his release from prison, London took the first train for Pennsylvania. During the ride, he thought about what had happened to him at the trial. He had not been permitted to speak in his own defense, and his frustrated demand for a lawyer had been greeted with laughter. Why, he had shouted, was he being locked up? What crime had he committed? If anything, the system itself was to blame. If he had been given a decent-paying job in Oakland, he would never have joined the Industrial Army, never starved, and never ended up in a dismal cell in the Erie County Penitentiary. It was all a vicious cycle, London decided, disgraceful in a country that claimed to be the richest, most democratic nation in the world. Something had to be done to change this injustice.

For the next several months, London tramped around the country, riding the boxcars, meeting other hobos, and listening to their stories of simple pleasures and supperless nights. All of these stories, these experiences, would lend a richness to London's later writing. Like author John Steinbeck, he caught the voice of the people—sometimes romantically, sometimes fiercely, always authentically. Years later, after London had become famous, hundreds of tramps would claim to have known him on the road, and their dubious stories became part of the Jack London myth. London himself could not remember individual names or faces, but the memories of cold nights, warmed by the laughter of strangers, stayed with him always.

Many of the hobos London met were educated men, self-styled teachers and philosophers, and, during his roaming, London listened to their conversations closely. It was during this period that he first heard the names of Karl Marx, Herbert Spencer, and Friedrich Engels, social thinkers who would later have a profound influence on his life. Listening to his fellow hobos discuss economics, philosophy, and sociology gave the 18-year-old a strange thrill, similar to the thrill he had felt guiding the *Sophia Sutherland* through the deadly typhoon. He wished he could add to the conversation, but what could he possibly say? He had never gone to high school, he knew nothing of Engels, Spencer, or the history of the American labor movement. London remained silent, but all the while he was thinking. He had already mastered the elemental force of a typhoon; now he wanted to master that more elusive beast, knowledge. And knowledge, he knew, could only come from one source: education.

Reluctantly, London turned west. He loved the carefree life of being a tramp, but it was also a desperate life, filled with hunger and cold and the constant fear of jail. Education, on the other hand, might give him the advantage he so badly needed. Over the years, London had tried his hand at many different types of manual labor, all of which had ended in failure. Working with his muscles alone obviously did not guarantee success. Now London was ready to try a different approach, and, making his way to Vancouver, he took a job as a coal stoker aboard the SS *Umatilla*, which eventually deposited him at the wharf of the Oakland estuary.

Returning to his mother's house on 22nd Avenue, London felt optimistic about the future. Oyster pirate, coal stoker, sailor, cannery worker, convict—these things were part of his past, not to be pursued again. Knowledge was the key now; book learning was the secret to success. Filled with high hopes, and with Flora's approval, London entered Oakland High School, enrolling in the winter class of 1897.

Buffalo, New York, as it appeared in the late 19th century. On June 19, 1894, London was convicted of vagrancy and imprisoned for 30 days in the Erie County Penitentiary in Buffalo. He neither forgot the horrors that he witnessed nor forgave the system that had put him there.

A team of sled dogs patiently waits to haul a prospector's gear over the forbidding arctic terrain. London rushed to the Klondike region of Canada when gold was discovered there in 1897.

4

The Klondike

"THEN," LONDON REMEMBERED, "began a frantic pursuit of knowledge." Setting up a small den in the back of his mother's cottage, he surrounded himself with piles of books from the Oakland Public Library. Sociology, language, economics, history, politics, science, mathematics—London was determined to learn as much as he could as quickly as he could. Speed was crucial. If, for some reason, he fell behind, the memory of the spinning bobbin at the jute mill spurred him on. Brains, not brawn, were the only thing that could save London from becoming a work beast.

He drove himself to the point of exhaustion, working 19 hours a day. As soon as he finished reading one book, he threw it aside and picked up another, hardly glancing at the clock and ignoring the hunger pains in his stomach. He considered sleep a nuisance; it robbed him of precious study time. Speed, speed! It became an obsession with London. Two years in high school, five more at the university—that was the plan. He would make whatever sacrifice was necessary to achieve his goal.

A cartoon lampoons the English social scientist Herbert Spencer. During his rigorous self-education campaign, London immersed himself in the writings of Spencer, the German socialist Karl Marx, and the English critic John Ruskin.

Five mornings a week, he rode his bicycle nearly 40 blocks to Oakland High School. From the start, his classmates shunned him. Children of the middle and upper classes, they were distrustful of London's baggy trousers, his lack of necktie, and the careless, jaunty angle at which he wore his cap. His hand-rolled cigarettes were shocking, and his socialist talk sounded dangerously radical. Most of all, they disapproved of London's intensity, his determination to perform at top speed, outshining everyone. The teachers, of course, admired his perseverance, but his peers wanted nothing to do with him.

If this bothered London, he did not let it show. As soon as school let out, he threw his book bag over his shoulder and pedaled home, eager to begin his afternoon of study. In addition to mathematics and sociology, he was reading a tremendous amount of literature: Herman Melville, Nathaniel Hawthorne, Richard Henry Dana, and Washington Irving. Though London was not yet planning to become a writer, he was nevertheless learning a great deal about writing. He appreciated, for instance, the importance of possessing a large vocabulary. Routine, uninspired writing could crush the heart and soul out of any sentence. As part of his program for self-improvement, London began memorizing as many new words a day as possible. He wanted his writing to sing, to jump; he wanted the reader to feel the sting of a harsh rain, smell the blubber on the decks of the sealing schooners.

Tentatively, he began sketching out scenes from his travels, which he submitted to the school magazine, the *Aegis*. To his surprise, they were immediately published. Seeing his work in print gave London tremendous encouragement, and gradually, over the course of the year, he earned the grudging respect of his fellow students. It was obvious to them that London had a talent for writing, even if they still had no intention of befriending him.

Hoping to broaden his knowledge, London began reading the philosophical works of Karl Marx, John Ruskin, and Herbert Spencer. He was especially interested in the latter, who celebrated individualism and, adopting the ideas of scientist Charles Darwin, advanced the brutal theory of "survival of the fittest." Increasingly, London found himself attracted to the principles of socialism. It seemed a solid, sensible form of government, and he began attending the outdoor meetings of the Socialist Labor party in City Hall Plaza. Mounted on soapboxes, orators would passionately condemn the evils of capitalism and, more often than not, praise the intelligence of Edward Bellamy's *Looking Backward*, the most influential utopian novel of the 19th century.

Socialism had not yet reshaped American government, and by the 1890s, it seemed unlikely that it ever would. In California especially, the party's goals were muddled and naive; the philosophy of Karl Marx and Friedrich Engels was largely unknown in the East Bay. London, nevertheless, was moved by the fiery speeches he heard in City Hall Plaza. Socialists such as Max Schwind and Frank Strawn-Hamilton advocated nothing less than immediate revolution. According to them, the exploitation of the common worker could no longer be tolerated; employees needed to organize and, with one decisive blow, destroy the system that was crushing them. This idea appealed strongly to London, and in April 1896, he joined the local branch of the Socialist Labor party.

Years later, in his novel *Martin Eden*, London summarized his reasons for signing up with the party: "As for me, you wonder why I am a socialist. I'll tell you. It is because socialism is inevitable; because the present rotten and irrational system cannot endure. . . . The slaves won't stand for it."

To London's distress, however, he had little time to devote to the cause. He was primarily a student, and he refused to let anything take him away from his studies. After a year at Oakland High School, however, he decided that the pace was too slow. Impatient to enter the university, London hit upon a different plan: He would drop out of school and teach himself, in the space of just four months, everything he needed to know to enter the University of California.

Day after day, isolated in his den, London remained hunched over his books, approaching his education with a single-mindedness that was almost frightening. "My body grew weary," he later admitted. "Perhaps, toward the last, I got a bit dotty." The hard work paid off, however. He passed his college examinations, and in the fall of 1896 he entered the University of California at Berkeley.

There he encountered bitter disappointment. For one thing, the classes seemed too slow. By now, London was used to working at his own furious pace, and he fully expected the university to encourage that pace. After a few weeks, it became painfully obvious to London that he was his own best teacher. He knew instinctively which subjects to pursue and which to avoid. He saw no purpose, for instance, in learning Latin or any other foreign language (a decision he would later regret). Dreaming vaguely of becoming a socialist writer, London enrolled in several English and composition courses, but he came away deeply disillusioned. Where was the passion, the thrill of acquiring knowledge? It did not seem to exist on the Berkeley campus.

London ended his first semester with serious doubts. Was it possible that he was wasting his time? What if the pace never picked up? He felt certain that if he applied himself, he could master nearly any subject. Would it be better to drop out once again and educate himself through the public library? Was a college diploma necessary to get a good job? These questions tortured London, and yet the students around him seemed perfectly happy. The freshman class had no intellectual hunger, no desire to overthrow the capitalist system. Bitterly, London realized that his classmates sought nothing more than a careful, measured existence—no risk, no glory. This angered him.

Books, he felt, should be a key to life, not a substitution for life itself.

In any event, London had reached the end of his patience. His classes were giving him neither pleasure nor stimulation, and, shortly after beginning his second semester, he dropped out with an honorary dismissal. His future was hardly secure, but that did not concern him at the moment. He was free now, free to do anything he wished.

For the next several months, London became quite active with the socialists, and, to his surprise, he frequently found himself mounting the soapbox at City Hall Plaza. The newspapers began calling him Oakland's "boy socialist," a young man with a passionate desire to improve the country's government. This small degree of fame,

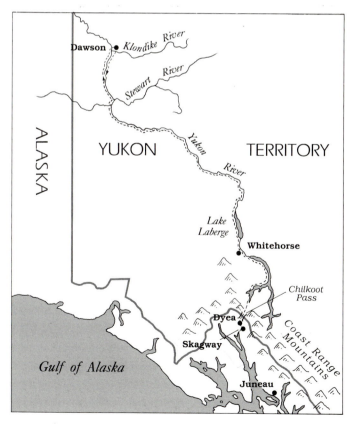

London's route to the Klondike.

however, brought unpleasant consequences. Eight days after leaving the university, London was arrested while speaking to the crowd. Remembering his previous arrest in New York, London stood up for his civil rights, demanding a trial by jury. After some deliberation, the city of Oakland dropped the case.

When he was not busy preparing speeches or attending meetings of the Socialist Labor party, London spent his time writing. Looking back, he remembered the period as one of the richest, most creative of his life: "Heavens, how I wrote! . . . The way I worked was enough to soften my brain and send me to a madhouse. I wrote, I wrote everything—ponderous essays, scientific and sociological, short stories, humorous verse, verse of all sorts from triolets and sonnets to blank verse tragedy and elephantine epics." This writing frenzy was performed upon a diabolical typewriter: "Its alphabet was all capitals. It was informed with an evil spirit. It obeyed no known laws of physics. . . . The keys of that machine had to be hit so hard that to one outside the house it sounded like distant thunder or some one breaking up the furniture."

By this time, London had more or less decided upon a writing career. That summer, though, an event occurred in San Francisco that would change his immediate future. The SS *Excelsior* sailed through the Golden Gate with the extraordinary news that gold had been discovered in the Klondike, a region in the Yukon Territory of northwestern Canada. Like a brushfire, the word swept across San Francisco, and, within a day, most of the nation was seized with excitement. For many years, it had been widely assumed that northern Canada was a barren wasteland; now, suddenly, it held out the promise of fabulous wealth, of irresistible danger, of the exploration of new, uncharted territory. The newspapers called it a modern odyssey, the last great adventure of the 19th century. Thousands responded to the call, abandoning their urban life and setting off for the great northern unknown.

Naturally, San Francisco was the logical point of departure. Overnight, a flood of gold seekers invaded the city, madly buying up whatever supplies were available. Without a job and with no desire to return to school, London allowed himself to be caught up in the frenzy. He and his brother-in-law, James Shepard, immediately borrowed what money they could and began packing for the long journey.

At that moment, Flora's husband, John, was near death, but young London could not be persuaded to stay at home. Too many people were leaving for Alaska, and London suspected that the goldfields would soon be exhausted. Hastily, he and Shepard threw together their outfit: heavy boots, shovels, picks, a map, tobacco, chewing gum, whiskey, food, sharp knives, books, mittens, long underwear, a used tent, and—carefully wrapped—a tremendous quantity of matches. Satisfied that they had forgotten nothing, London and Shepard bought their steamship tickets, and, on July 25, 1897, they sailed through the Golden Gate aboard the SS *Umatilla*, Klondike bound.

Nearly 500 men crowded the decks of the boat, all adventurers, all seeking a better life for themselves. During the week-long voyage, many of the men decided to form partnerships, and, before reaching Juneau, Alaska, London and Shepard had teamed up with three other miners: Merritt Sloper, "Big Jim" Goodman, and Fred Thompson.

Few of the men aboard the *Umatilla* suspected the hardships that awaited them in the Far North. The more practical ones, like James Shepard, realized their folly and turned back at Juneau. The majority, however, hired Tlingit Indian guides and paddled 100 miles upstream to Dyea, where they stared, speechless, at the indomitable Coast Ranges. It was here, at the foot of the infamous Chilkoot Pass, that the gold seekers had their first serious doubts. How on earth were they going to transport their baggage over that steep trail? Would their strength be sufficient to reach the top? London gave himself no time to think. He

In this 1897 drawing, Indian guides, carrying gold seekers and their gear, ford a river on the overland route to the goldfields in the Klondike. Because they could not afford to hire Indian porters, London and his mining partners carried their own gear over the mile-high Chilkoot Pass.

knew the importance of reaching Dawson before the winter freeze, and, struggling under the weight of their baggage, he and his partners fell in with the line of climbers ascending the steep, snowy pass.

The northern elements, the men discovered, were harsh. The weather at the bottom of the Chilkoot was unbearably hot, and, as London trudged upward, he began peeling off one layer of clothing after another. Stinging sweat ran into his eyes. At the half-mile point, many of the miners were on their hands and knees, gasping for breath. The wealthier men had hired Indians to help carry their baggage, but, at 40 cents per pound, this was a luxury London could not afford. To his dying day, he would never forget the sight of the Indians quietly passing him on the trail, bearing tremendous loads upon their backs. Deeply impressed by their strength of character, London forced himself to continue climbing. "To be almost as good as an Indian was a new ambition to cherish," he would later write.

By the time he reached the summit, the weather had turned to rain, making the path extremely slushy. London and his party were exhausted but in good spirits. The hardest part of the journey was now behind them, and, because of the downhill slope, it would be fairly easy to get to Lake Lindemann, where a large tent city had recently been established. It was at this point that the trail began thinning out. The ground had become swampy, and the exposed rocks were slick with ice. Ever mindful of winter's approach, London's party kept to a rapid pace, arriving at Lindemann on the afternoon of September 8. There they discovered a tempting array of goods for sale: hot meals, clean beds, boats, sled dogs, and knowledgeable Indian guides. London and his partners would not let themselves rest, however, and, heading a few miles upriver, they immediately began building a boat.

This was a wise move. Like most gold seekers, they were overloaded with supplies; London's baggage alone exceeded 1,500 pounds. A boat, then, was absolutely necessary if they wished to reach Dawson in Canada's Yukon Territory before the freeze. Working swiftly, the men finished the *Yukon Belle* within a matter of days, and, loading the craft, they set out on the next leg of their journey. Three lakes lay just ahead, the last of which, Lake Marsh, emptied into Fifty Mile River, which, in turn, would take them into the heart of the Yukon. Separating Lake Marsh and the river, though, was Box Canyon, which contained some of the deadliest rapids in the region.

Anchoring the *Yukon Belle*, London and his partners walked up and down the shore, studying the situation. Shooting the rapids was not going to be easy. For one thing, they were dangerously narrow, allowing little room for maneuvers. The water also appeared to be deep; if the boat capsized, it would be nearly impossible for the men to recover their outfits. The worst hazard, though, was the "Ridge," a foamy spot where the water apparently doubled back upon itself, rising to a height of nearly eight feet. Most of the miners avoided the rapids altogether, lugging everything on foot through the canyon. This would take at least two days, and, talking it over, London's group agreed they could spare neither the time nor the energy. Risking everything, they decided to tackle the rapids.

After securing all of the gear and taking their positions, they pushed the *Yukon Belle* into the swirling water. Word had spread quickly, and dozens of miners lined the banks of the canyon to watch the inevitable wreck. London had been elected captain, and, almost immediately, he could feel the strong pull of the white water. He tried desperately to steer, but the rapids had gripped the boat with ungodly force. At every moment, rocks sprang into view, beckoning disaster. Onshore, the miners were jumping up and down, frantically shouting directions.

Then, without warning, the boat began pitching violently: The *Yukon Belle* was on top of the "Ridge." London managed to ride it for several seconds; then, like a bronco, the water flipped the boat sideways, nearly capsizing it. It was all the men could do to hang on. They might easily have been battered to death against the rocks, but at the last moment, the craft shot forward, and, spinning around, they found themselves entering the calmer waters below the whirlpool. The men on shore went wild with hurrahs.

The *Yukon Belle* drifted along for nearly three miles before reaching the equally dangerous Whitehorse Rapids. Again, a fascinated crowd gathered to watch these foolhardy men risk their lives. Already caught in the swift water, London had only a few moments to take his bearings. The tricky part this time would be the "Mane of the Horse," a corkscrew nightmare of crashing waves. Gripping their oars, London and his crew disappeared into the foamy rapids. For a moment, it looked like the *Belle* had gone under, but no, up she came, clearing the waves with breathtaking splendor. London "rode the Horse" with supreme skill, safely landing the boat a few minutes later. Instantly, he was surrounded by men begging him to do the same for them. London and his partners were anxious to continue their journey, however, and London had to decline all offers.

Unfortunately, shooting the rapids had not saved them a great deal of time. The days were growing much shorter now—winter was approaching. By the time they reached Lake Laberge, it was already snowing; at least 100 boats were trapped in the icy water. London and his friends were now faced with a difficult decision: Camp here for the winter or press on toward Dawson? Rumors were circulating that most of the Yukon was already staked. Speed, therefore, was vital. For the next three mornings, London's men attempted to cross the lake, but each time they were driven back by the strong northern wind. The snow, meanwhile, was growing heavier; a blizzard seemed imminent. On the afternoon of September 28, they made their fourth attempt, launching the *Yukon Belle* into the frigid water. This time, they told each other, they would not turn back.

Progress was discouragingly slow. Every few minutes, a thick layer of ice formed on the oars and had to be chopped off with a hatchet. By nightfall, they were only halfway across the lake, but there could be no fire, no rest until they had won the northern shore. As the hours passed, London could feel the sensation in his fingers deadening; desperately, he beat them against his leg to restore circulation. His nose, exposed to the subzero air, went numb; his feet were leaden, difficult to move. Along the banks, the men could hear packs of wolves howling in the frozen solitude. Finally, toward dawn, they reached the mouth of the gushing Thirty Mile River. They did not know it, but the *Yukon Belle* was one of the last boats to escape Lake Laberge before the onset of winter.

During the winter of 1897–98, London lived in this cabin while he and his partners worked the claims that they had staked near Henderson Creek.

For more than a week, the men followed the river's course, gradually acclimatizing themselves to the bitter cold. During this time, they heard another disturbing

A group of pick-and-shovel men dig for gold in the Klondike. Looking back on his Yukon experiences, London observed, "I never realized a cent from any properties I had an interest in up there. Still, I have been managing to pan out a living ever since on the strength of the trip."

rumor. Dawson had grown so rapidly that it could not feed its 5,000 inhabitants. Famine was setting in. It seemed foolhardy to continue any farther, and a few days later, on October 9, London and his partners dropped anchor at Split-Up Island. By now, most of the Canadian rivers had frozen over, and they had little choice but to spend the next few months in this lonely spot.

Split-Up Island (also known as Upper Island) was located 80 miles from Dawson, between the Stewart River and Henderson Creek. To the men's surprise, the area had not yet been staked, and, by scouting around the creek, Jim Goodman discovered small traces of what appeared to be gold. Elated, the miners must have had visions of returning to San Francisco as wealthy men. They immediately moved into an abandoned cabin and began unloading their craft. A week later, London and Fred Thompson paddled to Dawson to register their claims.

Despite this promptness, London and Thompson were in no hurry to rejoin their partners to begin prospecting. They lingered in Dawson for nearly two months, warming themselves in the saloons and, when prices were low, stocking up on beans, flour, and bread. To pass the time, London gambled lightly at the roulette tables, and, if the mood was right, he would vigorously defend the merits of socialism. Most evenings, though, he sat quietly in one corner, listening to the old-timers spin their tales of near starvation, lost fortunes, blizzards, and faithful sled dogs. These stories enthralled London, and, years later, he would retell them powerfully in such books as *Children of the Frost*, *Smoke Bellew*, and, most popularly, *The Call of the Wild*.

In early December, London and Thompson returned by foot to Split-Up Island to begin prospecting. After a few days of backbreaking toil, the miners must have sensed the futility of their efforts. Most of the ground had frozen solid, trapping any gold for a minimum of six months. To complicate matters, it was perpetually dark. Sunlight lasted only a few hours each day, allowing little time for serious prospecting. These were difficulties the men had apparently not expected. Most troublesome, though, was the cold, and they spent a great deal of their time searching desperately for firewood. Warmth meant everything in the Yukon—without it, life ceased.

Not long after arriving at Split-Up Island, London received a letter from home telling him that his stepfather, John, had died on October 15. London's relationship with John had always been friendly, and this news, coming when it did, must have caused London some distress. Eight weeks before leaving for the Klondike, he had written to his natural father, William Chaney, asking him to explain the shocking story that he had discovered in the *San Francisco Chronicle*. Chaney's lengthy denial sounded

A Klondike prospector pans for gold.

suspicious, and now, sitting in his freezing cabin 80 miles from civilization, London must have been fighting not only the cold but more sinister adversaries: depression and self-doubt.

While waiting for the spring thaw, London gave a great deal of thought to his immediate future. It seemed unlikely that he and his partners would find their gold bonanza, and now, as the sole breadwinner of the family, it would be necessary for him to choose a career. But what talent did he have to offer? He was 22 years old, had dropped out of the university, and had never received any professional training. The only thing London had ever succeeded at was his writing, and even that victory was minor: a $25 first prize awarded by the *San Francisco Morning Call*. And yet, the idea of writing would not leave him. Sitting in his cabin one day, he used a pencil to scratch the following message onto the back wall: "Jack London. Miner, author. Jan. 27, 1898."

Shortly after this, London began noticing traces of blood in his spittle. Like most prospectors, his diet consisted largely of bacon, beans, and bread. Apparently, London did not realize that fresh vegetables were necessary to ward off scurvy, and by the time spring arrived, he was showing signs of the dreaded disease. His teeth, which had never been healthy, were even worse now, dangling loosely from their gums. The smallest tasks exhausted him, and, as his joints swelled up, paralysis set in. Whenever London pushed a fingernail into his skin, the dent remained. Obviously, he had to get to a doctor as quickly as possible.

In early May, the ice on the Yukon River began to break up. Dismantling their cabin, London's partners constructed a raft to carry him to Dawson. There London immediately checked himself into Father Judge's hospital, where he was put on a diet rich in vitamin C: onions, tomatoes, and lemon juice.

Usually, the effects of scurvy are quickly treated, but London's case proved troublesome. After a few weeks, the doctors advised him to abandon his claim at Split-Up Island and return to the States for further medical treatment. It must have been a painful decision—in a way, it made the entire trip pointless—but London did as he was told, floating 1,900 miles in a rowboat down the mosquito-ridden Yukon to St. Michael Island, Alaska. There he boarded the first of a series of vessels that eventually returned him to San Francisco.

It was during the trip down the Yukon that London first began jotting down his memories of the Klondike. By now, he firmly intended to become an author, and, like most young writers, London wanted to create grand, important works, novels and short stories that would stand the test of time. He was equally prepared, though, to write pure rubbish if that was what the public wanted. Anything to get his foot in the door, anything to save him from becoming a work beast.

Heading home, London felt defeated by the Klondike. Discouraged and in poor health, he did not realize that he was returning with a tremendous bonanza: the raw, bristling stories that would later become *White Fang*, *The Call of the Wild*, *Burning Daylight*, and *The Son of the Wolf*. Unlike most prospectors, London *had* discovered his fortune in the Yukon. It rested not along the banks of Henderson Creek but in the fertile soil of his own imagination.

London left this message on the back wall of his Klondike cabin: "Jack London. Miner, author. Jan. 27, 1898." After learning of the death of his stepfather and contracting a severe case of scurvy, he decided to return to San Francisco in June 1898.

Using a rock as a desk, Jack London works on a story outside the Wake Robin Lodge in the resort community of Glen Ellen, California.

5

Success

RETURNING TO HIS MOTHER'S COTTAGE on Foothill Boulevard, Jack London cleared a space at the kitchen table and hauled out his secondhand typewriter, the one that typed in capital letters. Flora must have watched him in silence. A practical woman, she could not have been pleased that her son had chosen such a competitive career as writing. Besides, the East Coast magazines were notoriously stingy, and even if London were lucky enough to sell two or three of his stories, the pay would not amount to more than $20 or $30, hardly enough to live on. No, Flora preferred quick, easy money, and during her son's absence, she had indulged herself in lottery tickets, positive that she would eventually win a small fortune.

London harbored no such delusions. He knew that hard work, not luck, was responsible for success, and a few days after returning to Oakland, he began writing down his experiences in the Yukon, trying to recapture the brutal, unflinching majesty of life in the northern wild.

From that day forward, writing became an absolute passion for London. Whenever he was at home, he could be found hunched over the typewriter, fighting his way through a Canadian blizzard; angrily whipping a team of hungry sled dogs; struggling desperately to build a fire with nothing more than wet twigs and a handful of sulphur matches. The quality of this early work may have been disappointing, but, at that moment, London was not concerned with quality. He wanted to fall into the rhythm of writing, to get used to the idea. To play critic at this point would only be self-defeating.

Of course, writing was not London's sole occupation. Times were hard, and it was vital that he find some sort of work to support himself and his 55-year-old mother. Unfortunately, the hardships of the depression of 1893 could still be felt in the West, and locating work was extremely difficult. "I had my name down in five employment bureaus," London remembered. "I advertised in three newspapers. I sought out the few friends I knew who might be able to get me work; but they were either uninterested or unable to find anything for me." In October, London passed an examination for the post office, but at the moment, he was told, there were no positions available. He would have to wait. Discouraged, he continued typing his tales of the Yukon.

It says a great deal about London's talent that only three months after returning home, one of his stories was accepted by the *Overland Monthly*, one of the West's most prestigious literary magazines. "To the Man on Trail" is considered today one of London's most successful stories, brimming with the drama and keen eye for detail that would fuel most of his later work. It also marked the first appearance of the Malemute Kid, who, from the security of his warm cabin, makes a memorable toast on a snowy Christmas Eve: "A health to the man on trail this night; may his grub hold out; may his dogs keep their legs; may his matches never miss fire." Obviously encouraged, London submitted a second, even better story to the *Monthly*, "The White Silence," which appeared in the February 1899 issue.

To London's disappointment, however, he was paid very little for his work: $5.00 for his first story, $7.50 for "The White Silence." It took no time for London to figure it out. "To the Man on Trail" had taken five days to write, which came out to exactly one dollar a day, the same wage he had earned at the cannery and the jute mill. Earlier, London had read that it was customary for magazines to pay at a rate of one cent per word. Obviously, this was not true—it was closer to one penny for every ten words. London doubted that he could survive on such wages. At the moment, he owed four dollars to the grocer and five to the butcher. His bicycle and winter coat had already been sent to the pawnshop, and his mother's rent was due in a few weeks. Discouraged, London saw no way out of his dilemma.

Then, providentially, he received a letter from *The Black Cat*, a Boston magazine, which offered him $40 for his short story "A Thousand Deaths." The editor's only stipulation was that it be shortened by 50 percent. London was too elated to quibble. This was excellent pay for a 2,000-word story, and, dashing to his typewriter, he wrote to the editor, telling him to send the money along. The acceptance of this horror story was important to London. It meant that he could stay in the writing game, at least for a few more months. "I was at the end of my tether," he wrote, "beaten out, starved. . . . Literally, and literarily, I was saved by the *Black Cat* short story."

It was about this time, coincidentally, that London received a letter from the post office informing him that a carrier position had become available at $65 a month. A few weeks earlier, London would almost certainly have accepted the job, but now, with Flora's approval, he called upon the postmaster and declined it. It must have been an awkward meeting, but London knew in his heart that he

The Black Cat, *a Boston magazine, published London's horror story, "A Thousand Deaths," in its May 1899 issue. The publication of this story provided London with the motivation and the money to continue his writing career.*

wanted to be an author, not a postman. It would be foolish, therefore, to give up his writing for the security of $65 a month. Taking his leave, London did not suspect how difficult, how supremely nerve-racking the next six months would be.

Without warning, the eastern magazines began rejecting his short stories. At first, London was bewildered, but, gradually, he came to realize that his writing was too raw and too shocking for most editors. Sentimental romance was the fashion of the day, and London's stories were rarely sentimental. Rejection slips clogged the mailbox. Frustrated, London speared them on a tall piece of wire; before long, the stack of paper was nearly five inches high. To complicate matters, he ran out of money for postage. London put everything he owned into hock, but the creditors were never satisfied. At one point, he and Flora had only five dollars between them. Beans and day-old bread became staples in the London household. Meat was an unheard-of luxury.

London's talent, however, was not completely overlooked. By June 1899, he had managed to sell a handful of pieces, including three stories to the *Overland Monthly*: "The Son of the Wolf," "The Men of Forty Mile," and "In a Far Country." The latter, especially, is one of London's masterpieces, a harrowing tale of two men struggling to survive in the Alaskan wilderness. It is generally agreed that no author has ever described the Klondike as powerfully as Jack London. He was fascinated by the primal laws of nature, by the harsh, inescapable "Code of the North." Again and again, his stories depict the Yukon as a vast, unconquerable territory, cruelly indifferent to man's presence. Only the strong survive the brutality of an Alaskan winter. The weak perish, destroyed by forces they cannot understand, cannot control.

By now, London was working a minimum of 16 hours a day. Every morning, whether he felt inspired or not, he forced himself to write at least 1,500 words. After a quick

An illustration from one of London's books chillingly depicts a pack of wolves on the prowl. London was fascinated by the primal laws of nature, and many of his stories and novels explore the struggle for existence among humans as well as animals.

lunch, he usually walked to the public library, where he spent several hours reading the literary magazines. This was no casual pastime. Like a scientist, London analyzed each short story, carefully studying its construction, its dialogue, its characters, its humor. What were its strengths? he asked himself. Its weaknesses? How could it be improved? He took copious notes, writing down every unfamiliar word. The next morning, while shaving, he repeated these words to himself, forcing them to become a natural part of his vocabulary.

Every night, London studied until two or three in the morning, boning up on the philosophy of Spencer, the biology of Darwin, the poetry of Dante and Walt Whitman, and the rise and fall of the Roman Empire. It was a grim, joyless schedule, but it got results. In October 1899, Boston's *Atlantic Monthly* purchased one of his short stories for the breathtaking sum of $120. Never before had London been so well paid for his writing. He immediately settled his debts, paid the landlord six months' rent in advance, and bought a new typewriter with the money left over.

"An Odyssey of the North," which was published in the January 1900 issue, is one of London's longest stories, a grim tale of an Aleutian Indian chief who spends the better part of his life searching the globe for his kidnapped bride. When he finally locates her, he discovers to his horror that she has become civilized, knowledgeable of the world, with no desire to return to the simple "dirty huts" of the Aleutian Islands. Moreover, she has fallen in love with her captor, a seven-foot yellow-haired superman of the North, a physical type who would obsess London for most of his career: "His chest, neck, and limbs were those of a giant. To bear his three hundred pounds of bone and muscle, his snowshoes were greater by a generous yard than those of other men. Rough-hewn . . . his face told the tale of one who knew but the law of might." In a final test of strength, the Aleutian chief has the pleasure of seeing his enemy die,

The young writer relaxes at his home in Oakland. By the age of 24, London had launched a promising writing career. National magazines were regularly publishing his Klondike stories, and his first book, The Son of the Wolf, *had received favorable reviews.*

but, sadly, it is an empty victory; he is unable to win back the love of his bride, who vengefully stabs him with her knife.

The publication of this story gave London a tremendous surge of self-confidence. Gathering together nine of his Klondike tales, he mailed them to the Boston publishing house of Houghton Mifflin, where they created a favorable stir. The editors were shocked by the brutality of London's writing, but they were also impressed by its strength and vigor. Here, they decided, was an author of startling originality. To London's relief, Houghton Mifflin offered to publish his stories the following spring in one volume entitled *The Son of the Wolf.* London could not sign the contract quickly enough. He had been writing professionally for only one year, and now he was signing on with one of the country's largest publishing houses—quite an achievement for a writer who had not yet reached his 24th birthday.

Looking back, it is surprising that *The Son of the Wolf* sold as well as it did. Victorian readers, enamored with the romances of Louisa May Alcott and F. Marion Crawford, were hardly prepared for London's realistic style of writing. A few daring authors, such as Stephen Crane and

Frank Norris, had rejected the sentimental, but their gritty books failed to change popular taste. The general public wanted its literature to be uplifting and polite; sordid realism was left to the Europeans. Frank Norris's *Mc-Teague*, which was published only one year before *The Son of the Wolf*, was lambasted by the critics, who called it ugly and worthless, "a monotony of brutality from beginning to end." Today, this vivid San Francisco novel is regarded as one of the finest examples of American naturalism.

With the dawning of the 20th century, however, there seems to have been a strong desire on the public's part to cast off the old and embrace the new. Within a short time, most of the conventional art forms—music, dance, and literature—would undergo tremendous changes, and such pioneers as dancer Isadora Duncan and composer Igor Stravinsky would command the cultural forefront.

The publication of London's book, then, could not have occurred at a better time. The stories in *The Son of the Wolf* fascinated Victorian readers. Relying heavily on his Klondike diary, London evoked with seeming ease the simple dignity of the northern Indians; the warm, jolly atmosphere of the Dawson saloons; the smell of fresh coffee at 30 below; even the taste of Yukon Christmas punch, a gut-stunning concoction of whiskey, brandy, and pepper sauce, enough to curl the toes of the hardiest sourdough.

The exotic quality of London's stories helped make *The Son of the Wolf* a solid, though not spectacular, success. One reviewer called London "a natural born story teller," whereas another predicted that London would eventually "take his place among the few writers of really international reputation."

Importantly, the book caught the attention of numerous magazine editors, who began requesting stories from the new "Kipling of the North," as London came to be called. Perhaps, these editors admitted, they had been too hasty in rejecting his previous submissions. London held no grudges and immediately sent off his most recent work, which began appearing with some regularity in magazines such as *Cosmopolitan* and *McClure's*. He also began working on his first novel, atmospherically titled *A Daughter of the Snows*.

Now that his name was becoming marketable, London had every reason to feel confident about the future. For some time, he had been toying with the idea of marrying and settling down; in fact, he had recently proposed to a delicate young woman named Mabel Applegarth. Mabel's mother, however, did not believe that London would ever be successful enough to support a wife and family and, to Mabel's distress, had broken off the engagement. Naturally, London was disappointed, but he did not give up the idea of marrying and having children. As he wrote to an acquaintance, he believed that marriage would turn him into "a cleaner, wholesomer man."

To achieve this end, he turned to Bessie Maddern, whom he had known casually for several years. Bessie (or Bess, as she was often called) was a mathematics tutor, attractive, forthright, a black-haired Irish lass with an appealing personality. From the very start, however, London felt no passion for her, nor did she feign any for him. Her fiancé, Fred Jacobs, had recently died, and now, in her mid-20s, Bess faced the unhappy prospect of spinsterhood. She must have been flattered, then, by London's interest in her. Well educated, she had read most of his short stories, and, though she found them rather shocking, she firmly believed that London would someday be a famous writer.

Aside from a mutual interest in photography, Bess and Jack had almost nothing in common. Apparently, this did not concern them. They felt happily relaxed in each other's presence, and, to avoid any misunderstanding, London made it clear to Bess that he was not seeking a wife so much as a helpmate, a companion, someone who would raise his children, cook his meals, clean house, and occasionally type his manuscripts. The arrangement, however odd it may have seemed to others, suited Bess and

Jack perfectly. After an extremely brief courtship, he proposed, she accepted, and they were married on April 7, 1900, the same day that *The Son of the Wolf* was published.

The marriage, predictably, was unhappy. For one thing, Bess did not get along with Flora, and the two-story house on East 15th Street was the scene of many violent arguments. Finally, tired of playing referee, London moved his mother into a cottage a few doors away, a decision that infuriated Flora.

A second, more serious problem was not so easily solved. Quite simply, Bess had no desire to associate with her husband's artistic friends. By this time, London had become the darling of Oakland's intellectual set, a Bohemian group that spent its Sunday afternoons picnicking in the hills of Piedmont, a small community adjacent to Oakland. These intellectuals—poets, painters, radicals—were clearly impressed by London's talent, and, after the publication of *The Son of the Wolf*, they began dropping by every Wednesday night for dinner, conversation, and lively card games. Bess did not fit in with this crowd, nor did she try, and after giving birth to a daughter, Joan, in January 1901, she retired into the background, where she was soon forgotten. (A second daughter, Bess—or Becky, as she was called—was born in October 1902.)

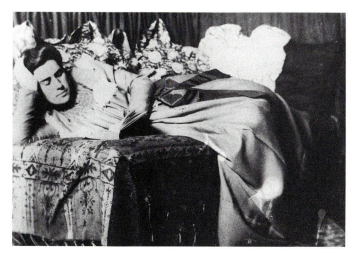

Bessie London reads one of Jack's books. London's first marriage, based more on friendship and convenience than on love, proved unhappy and ended in divorce in 1904.

In retrospect, it is not difficult to understand why London eventually decided to leave his wife. Bess, like Mabel Applegarth, was not imaginative. She did not share London's curiosity about the world, did not understand his reckless, adventurous spirit. "Above all," one of London's biographers has written, "she did not have her husband's sense of play and fun."

To be fully satisfied, London needed the presence of a vigorous, stimulating woman, someone who shared his passion for living. He found these qualities in Charmian Kittredge, a charming and athletic stenographer who frequently attended the Sunday afternoon picnics in Piedmont. Charmian was everything Bess was not—spirited, carefree, and refreshingly modern. She was one of the first

London visits his daughters Becky (left) and Joan (right). London always loved his children, but his relationship with the girls became distant and strained after he and Bess were divorced.

women in the Bay Area to ride a horse astride, not sidesaddle (a shocking breach of convention in 1901). Though it must have raised eyebrows, Charmian spent many afternoons with London, riding bicycles, playing horseshoes, swimming, and flying kites in the Oakland hills. On one occasion, she even slipped on a pair of boxing gloves and went several rounds with London, who delighted in this unconventional sparring partner.

Charmian was an avid reader, and, like Bess, she believed that Jack would someday be a famous author. During this period, London was struggling to finish his first novel, *A Daughter of the Snows*. He was also writing articles about the Klondike for the lucrative magazine market. His career took a healthy boost in 1901 when McClure, Phillips & Co. published his second collection of short stories, *The God of His Fathers*. By then, London was beginning to tire of Alaskan themes, and the stories, though well written, are not considered among his best. The critics, however, gave the book glowing reviews, calling London the "strongest short-story writer . . . since Poe."

Jack London's name was becoming so well known, in fact, that the Socialist party nominated him as the Oakland mayoral candidate in the 1901 election. London campaigned vigorously, but the citizens of Oakland were not ready for a Socialist mayor; London received fewer than 250 votes.

The following year, 1902, started off particularly well. In January, the Macmillan Company agreed to publish London's third collection of short stories, *Children of the Frost*. At the time, however, the Londons were nearly $3,000 in debt, and, before signing the contract, London requested a $200 advance. The money was promptly forwarded, and thus began London's long association with the Macmillan Company, which would publish nearly all of his books for the next 15 years. Unfortunately, London never learned to handle his money wisely, and instead of

Charmian Kittredge posed for this portrait in 1900, the same year that she met London.

London rests during a Bohemian Club gathering in 1904. Years later, London was disappointed when the Bohemian Club refused to stage his play, The Acorn Planter.

settling his debts, he and Bess immediately moved to a spacious new home in the Piedmont hills. The Bungalow, as they called it, was completely secluded, and, at $35 a month, a tremendous bargain.

For the relatively short time that he lived there, London was extremely happy in Piedmont. Friends dropped in constantly, and every Wednesday night, London found himself entertaining 15 or 20 people at a time. These were memorable gatherings, filled with laughter, party games, and lively debates. After supper, everyone would gather by the fire to hear London read from his latest work in progress. Of course, the Londons were living well beyond their means, falling ever deeper into debt. London must have been greatly relieved, then, when three of his books were published in the fall of 1902: *Children of the Frost*, a strong collection of Indian tales; *The Cruise of the Dazzler*, a forgettable—and forgotten—adventure story; and, finally, London's first full-length novel, *A Daughter of the Snows*.

This last book, according to most critics, is one of London's poorest. Awkwardly constructed, it is a novel of ideas, not action. Page after page, London's heroine, Frona Welse, battles her way across the northern landscape, but, too often, her actions are stiff and artificial, curiously bloodless. One critic has gone so far as to compare her to Frankenstein's monster, but, more accurately, Frona is London's fantasy of the perfect mate—someone, in fact, very much like Charmian Kittredge. Strong, courageous, and thoroughly independent, Frona is able to drive her sled dogs through the wildest of snowstorms. She is also an intellectual, and, repeatedly, London uses her as a mouthpiece for his own ideas about the natural supremacy of the Anglo-Saxon race. Most reviewers found *A Daughter of the Snows* tiresome, and even London privately admitted to a friend that it was "a failure."

Fortunately, his next book was more successful. London had only been living in the Piedmont house a few months when, unexpectedly, he received a telegram from the American Press Association (APA). The Boer War had just ended, and the APA wanted to know if London would be willing to go to South Africa to report on the postwar situation. It had been nearly four years since his return from the Yukon, and London was eager for a new adventure. Besides, Bess was pregnant with their second child, and the extra income would soon be needed. Jack immediately wired his acceptance.

Prior to his departure for England, however, he learned that the assignment had been canceled. Steamship ticket in hand, Jack decided to sail for London anyway, where he hoped to write an exposé on the city's slums. This was no whim; he had done extensive reading in the field of sociology, and he was curious to see for himself how bad the conditions really were in the East End.

Jack sailed aboard the RMS *Majestic*, arriving in England on August 6. After purchasing a pair of worn trousers and a tattered coat, Jack ventured into the worst quarter of London, where he carefully recorded the poverty and misery around him. The people of the East End, he observed, were wretched creatures, pinched with hunger and broken by years of toil in the factories. Success—even dignity—seemed impossible for these workers, their bodies ruined by disease, cheap meals, and too much liquor. "The London Abyss is a vast shambles. . . ." Jack wrote. "The color of life is gray and drab, everything is hopeless, unrelieved, and dirty."

Wandering the streets in his shabby clothes, he listened to the complaints of the ragpickers, the milliners, the ghetto children, the charwomen, even the foul-mouthed tarts who waited for sailors to pass. This unending chorus of anguish frustrated Jack: "Four hundred and fifty thousand human creatures," he concluded, "are dying miserably at the bottom of the social pit called East London."

For nearly two months, Jack inhabited the grimy East End, returning each night to his rented room on Dempsey Street to work on his manuscript. The resulting book, bleakly titled *The People of the Abyss*, was published by the Macmillan Company in the fall of 1903. Considering its grim subject matter, it received surprisingly good reviews, even from the British press, and today it remains one of Jack's most potent works. At the time of its publication, however, many critics accused the author of being too pessimistic. They felt that by focusing only on the filth and misery of the East End, Jack had written a lopsided book. This may be true, to some extent, but then again, it was not Jack's intention to write a comprehensive survey of London's social failings. Taken for what it is, *The*

People of the Abyss is a rousing success, one of the pioneering works of urban sociology.

Returning home from England, Jack stopped briefly in New York to meet with George Brett, the president of the Macmillan Company. During the course of their conversation, London informed Brett that he was tired of writing about the Klondike. His short stories had served him well, he admitted, but now it was time to tackle something "worthwhile," something of broader interest to the public. One week after returning to Piedmont, however, London began a second novel set in the frigid north, a robust story that many critics have come to regard as his finest literary achievement, *The Call of the Wild.*

It took London only 30 days to complete the story of Buck, a large, amiable dog enjoying a life of sloppy luxury on a prosperous California ranch. When gold is discovered in the Klondike, however, an immediate need arises for muscular sled dogs. Buck is kidnapped and sold by an

In this photograph taken by Jack London in 1902, indigent workers wait for food at the Salvation Army workhouse in London's East End. London dressed as a vagabond to conduct research for The People of the Abyss, *an account of the appalling social conditions in the slums of London, England.*

unscrupulous servant and, after a vicious beating, is transported by boat to the unfamiliar northern wilds: "He had been suddenly jerked from the heart of civilization and flung into the heart of things primordial. No lazy, sun-kissed life was this, with nothing to do but loaf and be bored. Here was neither peace, nor rest, nor a moment's safety. All was confusion and action. . . ."

In order to survive in this hostile environment, Buck is gradually forced to drop the ways of civilization and adopt "the law of club and fang," the harsh, bloody code that governs life in the Klondike. "His muscles became hard as iron. . . . Sight and scent became remarkably keen, while his hearing developed such acuteness that in his sleep he heard the faintest sound and knew whether it heralded peace or peril."

Throughout the novel, Buck is stirred by memories of his long-dead ancestors, "the wild-dogs [that] ranged in packs through the primeval forest and killed their meat as they ran it down." This instinctive yearning for "the old life within him" gradually becomes stronger until, in one memorable sequence, Buck feels driven to answer a distant, melancholy howl: "He sprang through the sleeping camp and in swift silence dashed through the woods. As he drew closer to the cry he went more slowly, with caution in every movement, till he came to an open place among the trees, and looking out saw, erect on haunches, with nose pointed to the sky, a long, lean, timber wolf."

The Call of the Wild was published by the Macmillan Company in July 1903. George Brett, the president of Macmillan, did not like the rough title, and, though he admired the book, he did not think it would do particularly well with the public, which favored sentimental animal stories such as Anna Sewell's *Black Beauty*. In lieu of royalties, Brett offered to buy the book for the flat fee of $2,000, promising to give it extensive promotion.

London had no reason to believe *The Call of the Wild* would become a best-seller, and, quite sensibly, he ac-

cepted Brett's offer. Financially, this was a mistake. The book sold out its entire first edition within 24 hours and has never been out of print since. If he had bargained for royalties, London would have become a wealthy man.

Throughout the country, critics showered the book with praise, calling it a "classic enriching American literature." The University of California was soon using it as a text in composition classes, and, for the first time in his career, London was regarded as an important figure in the literary world. Never again would he have any trouble selling his stories to a publisher. At the youthful age of 27, London had reached the top of his profession.

Sadly, he would always remember this particular period of his life with mixed emotions. The successful publication of *The Call of the Wild* was followed a few weeks later by the breakup of London's marriage.

While in Dawson, London camped in a tent beside the cabin of Marshall and Louis Bond. The Bonds' dog Jack (on the left) was the model for Buck in The Call of the Wild.

Clad in their waterproof oilskins, Jack and Charmian London pose in a photographer's studio before the launch of their 45-foot pleasure yacht, the Snark.

6

The Long Sickness

SHORTLY AFTER FINISHING *The Call of the Wild*, Jack London began having an affair with Charmian Kittredge, the lively stenographer with whom he had spent many Sunday afternoons picnicking in the hills of Piedmont. Charmian was five years older than Jack, an accomplished pianist, and an excellent horsewoman. Like London, she was filled with high spirits, always ready to laugh at a joke or plunge boisterously into a party game.

Jack admired Charmian for the very reasons that others disliked her. She was unafraid to speak her mind; she was ambitious; she was open to new ideas and new ways of doing things. Above all, she liked to think of herself as an emancipated woman. She made a point, for instance, of reading books that had been banned from the public library.

For Jack, Charmian represented freedom at a moment when he was feeling bored, even disgusted, with his marriage of convenience. Bess had many good qualities, but, in London's words, she was a woman with "a narrow band around her forehead," a dependable but rather dull person who did not believe in taking risks. Charmian, on the other hand, would not allow herself to be corseted by any Victorian notions of responsibility and behavior. She was a modern woman, outspoken, independent. "And," London later confessed to her, "there was a loneliness about you that appealed to me."

Their romance began in June 1903, while Bess and the girls were out of town. Jack had injured his knee in a buggy accident, and Charmian came to the house in Piedmont to comfort him. At first, their meetings were tender and discreet. "You cannot know how much you mean to me," London wrote. "The moments when first I meet you, and see you, and touch you, are unspeakably thrilling. . . ." Charmian's letters were equally passionate: "Think of me tenderly and lovingly and madly; think of me as your dear dear friend, your Sweetheart, your Wife. You are all the world to me. . . . Oh, Jack, Jack!"

By the end of July, London seems to have lost all interest in continuing his marriage. One day, after an intense four-hour conversation with Charmian, he went to his wife and said abruptly, "Bessie, I am leaving you." Bess was devastated. She begged for an explanation, but London would tell her nothing. Of course, she eventually learned that he was having an affair with Charmian, and this, too, was deeply wounding, because she had come to regard Charmian as one of her closest friends. This dual betrayal left her deeply bitter, and in the years to come, Bess could never forgive Jack for his unexpected desertion.

After packing his belongings, London moved to a spacious flat on Telegraph Avenue in Oakland. Naturally, he was distressed at the idea of abandoning his family, but, writing to a friend a few weeks later, he decided that, all in all, "I have performed what I consider the very highest of right acts." The Londons' separation and eventual divorce were widely covered by the national press. London was, after all, the author of *The Call of the Wild* and therefore a public celebrity.

For the next several months, Jack and Charmian tried to keep their relationship a secret, rarely meeting more than twice a week. Throughout the summer and fall, however, they exchanged dozens of passionately soggy love letters. Jack to Charmian: "When I say I am your slave, I say it as a *reasonable* man—which goes to show how really and completely mad I am." Charmian to London: "Ah, my love, you ARE such a man. And I love you, every bit of you, as I have never loved, and shall never love again!" On one occasion, Charmian paid a consoling visit to Bess and the children, but she left feeling understandably guilty. "Sometimes," she confessed to London, "I have to fight off a feeling of actual WICKEDNESS."

Though his letters to Charmian might not suggest it, Jack was now at the very height of his creative powers.

This Japanese lithograph depicts a battle of the Russo-Japanese War. London reported on the war for the San Francisco Examiner *but returned to the United States when he became exasperated by the restrictions imposed by the Japanese government, which prevented him from writing firsthand accounts of the conflict.*

Remembering his voyage on the *Sophia Sutherland*, he decided to write a vivid sea epic, a plan that George Brett enthusiastically supported. In order to put himself in the proper mood, London used part of his earnings from *The Call of the Wild* to purchase a small sailboat, the *Spray*, upon which he spent the better part of the summer cruising the backwaters of northern California.

This was a completely satisfying way of life for London. Yielding to his wanderlust, he felt free, unbridled, potent. Life, he sensed, was an exhilarating adventure, if one only had the courage to make the most of it. "There is an ecstasy," London wrote, "that marks the summit of life and beyond which life cannot rise." In the best of his writing, London attempted to capture and preserve that ecstasy (or, as he once vigorously called it, that "tidal-wave of being").

London had nearly completed his epic, *The Sea-Wolf*, when he received an offer from the Hearst press to go to Japan to cover the impending Russo-Japanese War. At the moment, London was broke, and he quickly accepted Hearst's offer, sailing for Yokohama on January 7, 1904.

The trip proved to be a bureaucratic nightmare. Upon arriving in Tokyo, London learned that the Japanese government had no intention of letting the correspondents go anywhere near the Manchurian battlefront. London was determined to get his story, however, and striking out on his own, he sailed up the "wild and bitter" coast of Korea to Chemulpo, a port city near Seoul. From there, he managed to penetrate deep into the heart of Manchuria, sending out numerous dispatches and dozens of photographs. When his envious colleagues got wind of what was happening, they demanded that their brash rival be recalled at once. For the rest of the war, London was kept safely behind the lines, carefully watched by Japanese officials. "[I am] profoundly irritated by the futility of my position," he wrote to Charmian. "Only in another war, with a white man's army, may I hope to redeem myself."

Unfortunately, London had gone to Japan with mixed feelings about the Japanese people and their culture. Viewing a group of Russian prisoners behind Japanese bars, he could not help sympathizing with the robust cossacks. "These men were my kind," he wrote in one of his dispatches, declaring that he would prefer to join the Russians "in their captivity, rather than [remain] outside in freedom amongst aliens."

When these anti-Japanese dispatches were published in the United States, many people, including London's fellow socialists, were shocked. The Socialist party was opposed to racial prejudice, and when London was reminded of this several months later, he pounded his fist on a table, exclaiming, "I am first of all a white man and only then a socialist!"

Disgusted by his inability to cover the Russo-Japanese War and anxious to resume his relationship with Charmian, London returned to San Francisco on June 30, 1904. Three months later, his novel *The Sea-Wolf* was published by the Macmillan Company. Like *The Call of the Wild*, it became an immediate best-seller, the critics praising it as a work of "rare and original genius."

A thrilling adventure, *The Sea-Wolf* begins rousingly with the foggy collision of two vessels in the San Francisco Bay. Among those tossed overboard is the narrator, Humphrey Van Weyden, who is rescued from the chilly waters by Wolf Larsen, the captain of a mysterious seal schooner bound for Japan. Larsen, a savage, domineering beast, is one of London's finest, most complex creations, and his subsequent conflict with the weakling Van Weyden forms the heart of this brutal Darwinian novel.

Naturally, Van Weyden distrusts and fears Larsen, and yet, at the same time, he is mesmerized by the captain's physical perfection: "I had never before seen him stripped, and the sight of his body quite took my breath away. . . . [His] great muscles leaped and moved under the satiny

After the success of The Call of the Wild *(1903), London's publisher ran this advertisement in the* Atlantic Monthly *to promote* The Son of the Wolf, *a collection of stories originally published in 1900.*

By **JACK LONDON**
The Son of the Wolf

"Sons of the Wolf, the Indians of the far North call the invading, conquering, devouring white man." And Mr. London's story is dedicated "To the Sons of the Wolf who sought their heritage and left their bones among the shadows of the Circle."

"Nature has many tricks wherewith she convinces man of his finity — the ceaseless flow of the tides, the fury of the storm, the shock of the earthquake, the long roll of heaven's artillery — but the most tremendous, the most stupefying of all is the passive phase of the White Silence."

Author of "The Call of the Wild"

Selections from the newspaper reviews.

"It is to be doubted if Kipling ever wrote a better short story than 'The Son of the Wolf.'" — *Kansas City Star.*
"You cannot get away from the fascination of these tales once you have dipped into them and caught a glimpse of this life, so unlike the life of any other country on the globe." — *San Francisco Chronicle.*
"These stories are realism, without the usual falsity of realism." — *N. Y. Times.*
"Mr. London has a fresh field, and a wonderful field. He has, too, a most uncommon power of his pen, a deep, strong, true feeling, and a notable dramatic instinct." — *The Interior*, Chicago.

With frontispiece and decorative holiday binding, price $1.50

Houghton, Mifflin and Company, Boston and New York

skin. . . . I stood motionless, a roll of antiseptic cotton in my hand unwinding and spilling itself down to the floor."

Shortly after this taut passage, London feels compelled to introduce a woman into the plot, and, for many readers, it is precisely at this point that the novel becomes less believable. *The Sea-Wolf* is primarily a story of masculine struggle, and the presence of "delicate, ethereal" Maud

Brewster cannot help but seem out of place. The inevitable romance between Brewster and Van Weyden is at once silly and artificial, weakening to some extent what many critics consider to be an otherwise perfect book.

It was after the publication of *The Sea-Wolf*, in the late fall of 1904, that Bess was granted a divorce from Jack on the grounds of desertion. The two children, Joan and Becky, were placed in their mother's custody, and, as part of the settlement, London agreed to buy a lot on 31st Street in Oakland and build a house upon it for the family. Flora, meanwhile, hastened to assure the *San Francisco Chronicle* that her son was not to blame for the breakup: "I do not recall where Jack once said an unkind word to her or did anything that could in any way hurt her feelings. He was loving, affectionate and generous to a fault." Be that as it may, it was a bitter, highly publicized split, and, among other things, it seems to have thrown London into a period of deep depression—his "long sickness," he later called it.

In his semi-autobiographical book *John Barleycorn*, London tried to explain the source of this melancholy. Apparently, he had reassessed his career and, in doing so, came to the sad conclusion that he had been betrayed by his ideals, by everything he had striven to achieve as a writer. "The things I had fought for and burned my midnight oil for, had failed me," he wrote. "Success—I despised it. Recognition—it was dead ashes." Even his love for Charmian seems to have ebbed during this period. Searching for new fulfillment, he stepped up his socialist activities, lecturing before a wide variety of groups. London even allowed himself to be talked into running for mayor again, and, to everyone's surprise, the author of *The Sea-Wolf* received nearly 1,000 votes—not enough to win but a big advance over his previous campaign in 1901.

It was also during this period that London's health began to bother him. He developed an excruciating itch; he feared he had a tumor on his rectum; he found it difficult to sleep. A profound feeling of disgust darkened every thought, every action: "I meditated suicide coolly, as a Greek philosopher might. . . . So obsessed was I with the desire to die, that I feared I might [shoot myself] in my sleep, and I was compelled to give my revolver away." In an effort to regain his mental health, London temporarily moved to the resort community of Glen Ellen, a secluded spot north of San Francisco. It was here, removed from the pressures of daily life, that he finally began to recover his peace of mind.

Fortunately, London's various illnesses do not seem to have affected the quality of his writing. In 1905, the Macmillan Company published three of London's books, including *The War of the Classes* (a collection of revolutionary essays) and *The Game*, a short, grim novel about prize fighting. *The Sea-Wolf*, meanwhile, was still selling well, and that summer London decided to use some of his royalties to purchase a beautiful estate in Glen Ellen. The Hill Ranch, as it was called, was located at the base of Sonoma Mountain, in the Valley of the Moon, and consisted of 129 acres of redwoods, natural springs and lush vegetation. Though he could not afford it, Jack bought the land for $7,000, explaining to Charmian that, after their marriage, they would move to Glen Ellen permanently.

Needless to say, the purchase of this ranch left London completely broke. To raise money, he immediately sat down and began writing another dog story, a long companion piece to *The Call of the Wild*. This time, however, he chose to reverse the process: "I'm going to give the evolution, the civilization of a dog—development of domesticity, faithfulness, love, morality." Comparisons between the two novels were bound to arise, and, indeed, *White Fang* has never enjoyed the popular acclaim of its predecessor. Perhaps it has to do with the plot—the process of domestication, after all, is bound to be anticlimactic. It would be wrong, however, to regard this as a defect of the novel. *White Fang* is extremely well written, utterly convincing, and, in its fiercer moments, every bit as gripping as its celebrated predecessor. "No stronger piece of work in this field has appeared," said the *New York Independent.*

It was during the writing of this novel, coincidentally, that London himself was becoming domesticated. He and Charmian were very happy in the Valley of the Moon, and, contented, they spent the autumn of 1905 galloping on horseback across the rolling hills of manzanita (a variety of evergreen shrub). Playing the gentleman farmer, London ordered the construction of a new barn. He also partially blocked a nearby creek to form a swimming hole. "I am anchoring good and solid," he wrote to a friend, "and anchoring for keeps." It was also at this time that Jack first began discussing with Charmian a trip he wanted to take, a seven-year voyage around the world. An experienced sailor, he could see the yacht clearly in his mind—45 feet long, 3 staterooms, a powerful engine, modern bathroom, copper sheathing, and all the latest nautical equipment. Charmian seized upon the idea, and many lazy afternoons were spent planning the voyage.

The only obstacle, as far as London was concerned, was the cost—the construction of the boat alone would run close to $7,000. To raise the necessary funds, London arranged to spend the next several months touring the Midwest, lecturing on the inevitability of socialism. Fortunately, his timing was perfect. The socialists had done surprisingly well in the last presidential election, and, as a well-known author, London was widely regarded as the party's leading spokesman. Not everyone applauded his commitment to the cause, however. "London is no Socialist," thundered one San Francisco paper. "He is a firebrand and red-flag anarchist, by his own confession . . . and he should be arrested and prosecuted for Treason."

Naturally, people were curious to see this firebrand in person, and the first weeks of the tour were highly successful. Every lecture was well attended, and provincial reporters fought for the chance to interview America's most

This portrait of London was taken in January 1906. That year, London devoted much of his time to supervising the construction of the Snark.

famous socialist. Then, inadvertently, London embroiled himself in a scandal that would tarnish his reputation for years to come. He was lecturing in northern Ohio when he received a telegram on November 18 informing him that his divorce from Bess had become final. It would have been customary, and proper, to have waited a few months before remarrying. London, however, had no patience for such niceties. Within 24 hours, he and Charmian were wed by a Chicago justice of the peace.

The wedding touched off an immediate scandal. Newspapers throughout the nation expressed shock at the "indecent haste" of the marriage. London's morality was

Fires rage out of control following an earthquake that devastated San Francisco on April 18, 1906. As a result of the earthquake, the price of building materials and labor soared, increasing the construction costs of the Snark *and delaying its completion.*

openly condemned by numerous social groups; a few libraries went so far as to remove his books from their shelves. Charmian, who had thus far managed to escape publicity, was suddenly being lambasted as that "ugly-faced girl from California." In the wake of such public outcry, the lecture tour began to collapse. London's rabble-rousing brand of socialism was now viewed as distinctly un-American, and it was only a matter of weeks before he had to cancel the rest of his engagements. Deeply discouraged, he and Charmian beat a hasty retreat to California, where work had just begun on their 45-foot pleasure yacht, the *Snark*.

For the next 14 months, the construction of this boat proved to be an unending source of frustration. In retrospect, it might have been cheaper and less aggravating if London had purchased another craft and begun the voyage at his own convenience. In 1906, however, there were very few vessels that would have met his specific needs, and besides, he had already signed a contract with *Cosmopolitan* magazine to write a story about the building of the boat. Brashly, London declared that the *Snark* would be the finest yacht ever constructed in San Francisco.

On the very day that the iron keel was to be laid, however—April 18, 1906—the Bay Area was shaken by a cataclysmic earthquake. The Londons were fast asleep at Glen Ellen when the first tremor hit at 5:13 A.M. Throwing on their clothes, they mounted horses and took a quick

A photograph taken by Jack London shows the damage caused by the earthquake.

survey of the property for damage. Then, making their way to Oakland by train, they boarded the first ferry for San Francisco to see for themselves the extent of the destruction.

Most of the city, they discovered, lay in ruins. The buildings that had not been toppled by the quake were being rapidly destroyed by the raging fire that followed. "San Francisco is gone," London wrote somberly. "Nothing remains of it but memories."

Naturally, the cost of labor and materials immediately skyrocketed. For nearly a year, wood remained something of a rarity, and London was forced to pay dearly for the ongoing construction of the *Snark*. His original budget of $7,000 proved insufficient and was swiftly doubled. To meet the spiraling expenses, London threw his pen into high gear, turning out numerous magazine articles and short stories. These included "The Wit of Porportuk," an Alaskan tragedy, and "The Apostate," a harrowing recollection of his days in the jute mill.

It was also during the summer of 1906 that London began writing *The Iron Heel*, which is today considered one of his finest achievements in fiction. A seething attack on capitalism, *The Iron Heel* is set in Chicago, several centuries in the future. There, in an overcrowded commune, the "raging, screaming" masses futilely attempt to throw off their oppressor, an evil oligarchy determined to crush labor resistance. In one scene, the government's intentions are made chillingly clear: "We will grind you revolutionists down under our heel, and we shall walk upon your faces. The world is ours, we are its lords, and ours it shall remain."

Certainly, *The Iron Heel* is one of London's bleakest, most prophetic books, and when it was published in 1908 it was largely ignored by the press, which considered it too radical and too pessimistic. Thirty years later, however, with the rise of Fascism in Europe, the book was given renewed attention. Russian revolutionary Leon Trotsky was deeply impressed by its "historical foresight"; biographer Irving Stone called it "one of the most terrifying and beautiful books ever written." Sadly, *The Iron Heel* seems to have fallen out of favor in recent years; it remains, nevertheless, a riveting, highly contemporary novel and a classic in the field of political fiction.

By the time London completed the book in December 1906, he was busier than ever planning his round-the-world voyage. It was to be a leisurely cruise, he told one magazine: "I calculate that seven years at least will be taken up by the trip." Construction on the *Snark*, meanwhile, was proceeding at a snail's pace, the victim of "inconceivable and monstrous" delays. To some degree, of course, difficulties were to be expected. London was dealing with more than 100 firms, none of which felt obliged to deliver their materials on time. Every month seemed to bring some new setback, and by the start of the new year London was feeling extremely frustrated. "I won't be happy until I get away," he told the editor of *Woman's Home Companion*. "And I'm going to get away as fast as God, earthquakes, and organized labor will let me."

To complicate matters, the *Snark* was accidentally damaged while she lay in the Oakland estuary. During an evening squall, two lumber scows collided against London's boat, seriously weakening her sides; by morning, the *Snark* was no longer airtight. Fed up with these endless delays, Jack and Charmian decided to sail to Hawaii and finish the boat there, where the costs of labor and materials would be much cheaper.

The Londons' departure from Oakland on the morning of April 23, 1907, was a great event, with horns blowing, flags waving, and hundreds of people cheering loudly on the docks. All told, $30,000 had gone into the construction of the *Snark*, and as London sailed out to sea, the wind whipping his hair, he saw himself as one lone man pitted against the "great natural forces." This, he sensed, would

London, always gregarious and fun-loving, strikes a mock serious pose with a painted cutout.

Jack and Charmian conduct a final inspection of the Snark, *which was launched on April 23, 1907. London boasted that the seven-year round-the-world voyage would be the greatest adventure of his life.*

be the grandest, most satisfying adventure of his life. Naturally, London felt discouraged when things began to go wrong. Within hours, the bathroom had ceased to function; the navigator, Roscoe Eames, quietly admitted he did not know how to navigate; Charmian and the rest of the crew became violently seasick.

Then, halfway to Honolulu, the $30,000 *Snark* began to leak—badly. Salt water rushed into the damaged compartments, ruining the tools and most of the food. Fuel seeped out of the gasoline tanks; a large amount of coal was swept overboard; the 70-horsepower engine failed to run. Daily pumping was required to keep the *Snark* afloat, and, as London later put it, "More trust could be placed in a wooden toothpick than in the most massive piece of iron to be found aboard."

By the time the Hawaiian Islands drifted into view, on May 17, everyone was physically and emotionally exhausted. Dropping anchor, the *Snark* put in for completion, and after firing Roscoe Eames, Jack and Charmian abandoned themselves to what she called the "blissful tent-and-surf life at Waikiki."

The five-month Hawaiian layover was extremely pleasant, the most untroubled portion of the whole voyage. London spent his mornings writing travel articles and short pieces of fiction; he also worked steadily on a new novel, *Martin Eden*. His afternoons were spent swimming, canoeing, surfboarding, and—whenever possible—sightseeing. One of his most interesting side trips was a week-long visit to the notorious leper colony at Molokai. Leprosy, at that time, was believed to be highly contagious, and anyone infected with the mysterious disease was banished to this remote isle. London, however, remained unafraid, mixing freely with the "horribles," as he called them. Later, he wrote a tragic story about the plight of the lepers as well as a highly sympathetic account of Molokai for *Woman's Home Companion*.

Charmian, meanwhile, kept an extensive journal of her own, which was later published in two volumes, *The Log of the Snark* (1915) and *Our Hawaii* (1917). Jack, too, recorded his own account of the voyage in *The Cruise of the Snark* (1911). These books describe in great detail their joyful departure from Hawaii; the *Snark*'s lonely, hazardous passage to the distant Marquesas Islands; the wretched, tubercular natives of the valley of Typee; one crew member's humorous attempt to win a bet by eating 20 bananas in half an hour (he failed); an unusual Christmas feast made up of shrimp fritters, fried taro, and sliced oranges with grated coconut. Throughout the voyage, Charmian tried to stay as cheerful as possible. She could not help revealing in her log, however, the ever-mounting frustrations that would eventually bring the cruise to its premature end.

The bedding, for instance, was continually damp and usually infested with cockroaches and centipedes. The flour tin, it was discovered, harbored a colony of weevils and black bugs. The 70-horsepower engine, which was supposed to have been repaired in Hawaii, broke down again, leaving the *Snark* at the mercy of uncooperative winds. "And while I am about it," London recalled with disgust, "I may as well confess that the five-horse-power, which ran the lights, fans, and pumps, was also on the sicklist." Gradually, Charmian noticed, the staterooms were taking on "a disagreeable odour of staleness and mouldiness." One morning, she reached for the wrong bottle and accidentally brushed her teeth with ammonia, searing her mouth for days. To everyone's horror, one-half of the supply of fresh water was lost. Letters from home indicated that London's affairs were being handled disastrously.

And then, most seriously, there were the illnesses. The list of ailments that Jack, Charmian, and the crew had to contend with was formidable: toothache, stomachache, headache, cholera, malaria, diarrhea, mosquito bites, boils, ulcers, burns, cuts, infections, sores, fever, and dysentery. Relying on medical textbooks, London tried his best to keep everyone healthy; jokingly, he called himself the "Amateur M.D." His diagnoses, however, were not always successful. In an attempt to heal some painful sores on his rectum, London administered daily doses of corrosive sublimate, an extremely dangerous medication that probably shortened his life.

By September 1908, the *Snark* had become a floating hospital. Charmian was in the throes of a bad fever, and

Jack was suffering a severe case of yaws, a tropical disease that covered his face, hands, and feet with unsightly lesions. Then, to his alarm, his hands began swelling to twice their normal size. "It hurts him to close them," Charmian wrote, "and the skin peels off in patches, with other skins readily forming and peeling underneath. I do not believe his nervous system was ever made to thrive in the tropics." By now, it seemed clear to everyone that London was too ill to continue the voyage. As soon as it could be arranged, he and Charmian took the first boat to Sydney, Australia, where Jack checked himself into the hospital for immediate treatment.

Unfortunately, the doctors could do little to relieve his mysterious skin condition. "It was unknown in the literature of medicine," London wrote. At one point, the "Amateur M.D." became convinced that he was suffering from leprosy, but the doctors assured him that he was mistaken.

Jack and Charmian stayed in Australia for nearly five months. Although Jack's health gradually improved, he and Charmian decided, on December 8, to call off the rest of the voyage. One by one, the crew members drifted away, and according to Charmian, the *Snark* was eventually sold to an English syndicate operating in the New Hebrides. The Londons never saw the boat again.

During the ill-fated voyage of the Snark, *London uses a sextant, a common navigational device, to determine the yacht's location.*

*London enjoys a relaxing trot across the Beauty Ranch. After return-
ing from the disappointing* Snark *voyage, London devoted much of his
energy to improving his ranch, located in Glen Ellen, California.*

7

The Beauty Ranch

DURING THE VOYAGE of the *Snark* and the subsequent period of sickness and recovery, London completed two novels, *Adventure* and *Martin Eden*. He also wrote numerous short stories, including "To Build a Fire" and "A Piece of Steak." The first is a masterful tale of Klondike despair, the second a deeply moving portrait of a broken-down prize-fighter.

Adventure, published in 1911 by the Macmillan Company, is a forgettable South Seas melodrama, written at the height of London's physical suffering. For good reason, it has been dismissed by critics as one of his worst stories. *Martin Eden*, however, is a triumph, a novel that has influenced many generations of writers and is now considered to be among the strongest books Jack London ever wrote.

Passionately autobiographical, it tells the story of a young Oakland sailor who overcomes tremendous obstacles to become a world-famous writer. Along the way, however, Martin grows hopelessly disillusioned, despising not only his success but the so-called intellectuals who seek him out, the bourgeoisie who continually flatter him with their stupid praise: "[T]hey were numskulls, ninnies, superficial, dogmatic, and ignorant. . . . What was the matter with them? What had they done with their educations? They had had access to the same books he had. How did it happen that they had drawn nothing from them?"

In his despair, Martin flees from society, sailing for the South Pacific, where he hopes to find a simpler, more satisfying existence. By then, however, it is too late. Love, money, socialism, friendship, success—they are all worthless to Martin Eden because he has lost his faith in mankind. "He saw, clear eyed, that he was in the Valley of the Shadow. . . . Life was to him like strong, white light that hurts the tired eyes of a sick person. . . . It hurt. It hurt intolerably." Martin's agony at last becomes unbearable, and, crawling out of his porthole, he plunges into the chilly depths of the Pacific Ocean:

Working outdoors, London puts the finishing touches on one of his stories. Observing a rigid schedule, London produced an astounding number of manuscripts after 1909. Although much of his writing during this period lacked the quality of his earlier work, he produced several distinguished novels and short stories, including The Star Rover *and "The Mexican."*

Down, down, he swam till his arms and legs grew tired and hardly moved. He knew that he was deep. The pressure on his ear-drums was a pain, and there was a buzzing in his head. His endurance was faltering. . . .

Colors and radiances surrounded him and bathed him and pervaded him. What was that? It seemed a lighthouse; but it was inside his brain—a flashing, bright white light. It flashed swifter and swifter. There was a long rumble of sound, and it seemed to him that he was falling down a vast and interminable stairway. And somewhere at the bottom he fell into darkness. That much he knew. He had fallen into darkness. And at the instant he knew, he ceased to know.

Unfortunately, *Martin Eden* had little success when it was published in 1909. The book was criticized for being entirely too pessimistic. Why, readers wondered, should it have been necessary for a popular writer like Martin to commit suicide? Some critics went so far as to suggest that London had burned himself out as an author. This, of course, was not true—the quality of writing in *Martin Eden* is unusually high. It cannot be denied, however, that after his return from Australia, London used his talent solely as a means to make money. "I prefer living to writing," he insisted, and during his lengthy convalescence, London devoted most of his energy to improving and expanding his estate at Glen Ellen.

The Beauty Ranch, as it came to be called, encompassed nearly 1,100 acres by the spring of 1910. Ambitiously, London told everyone that he was going to turn it into a model of productivity, one of the most profitable working ranches in the region. Horses and cattle were brought in, fields were gradually cleared, and, at great expense, more than 100,000 eucalyptus trees were planted, an investment that London believed would someday earn him a sizable fortune. He also took this opportunity to invite his stepsister Eliza to move to Glen Ellen to oversee his affairs.

Eliza, now separated from her husband, James Shepard, accepted Jack's offer, and for the next 29 years she served as the superintendent of the Beauty Ranch.

During this period, London also hired an architect to draw up blueprints for an enormous stone house he wanted to build at the northwest edge of the property. The 26-room Wolf House was to be fashioned entirely out of redwood and volcanic stone, and as soon as the necessary rocks were quarried, construction began in April 1911.

Since their dream home would not be finished for at least two years, the Londons temporarily moved into a small, informal ranch house near the center of the property. Here London resumed the open house policy that had proved so popular at the Bungalow in Piedmont. "The latchstring is always on the outside at the Beauty Ranch," he wrote at the bottom of all his correspondence. "Come visit us, and stay as long as you like." Needless to say, hundreds of friends and acquaintances were soon taking the train for Glen Ellen, anxious to spend a few days—or a few weeks—with the famous author. London was a generous host, and no one, it seems, was ever turned away. Socialists, writers, intellectuals, musicians, actors, farmers, professors, and even raggedy hobos from London's tramping days managed to find their way to the Sonoma estate.

On the whole, the next few years were among the most satisfying of London's life. His books were selling well, he was learning a great deal about ranching, and he and Charmian were constantly surrounded by good friends. Nights at the ranch house were alive with laughter and festivity, music, and lively conversation. Food and drink were abundant, and after supper Jack and Charmian would entertain their guests with hair-raising stories of their adventures on the *Snark*. Then, if the weather was warm, London would load everyone into a large wagon and drive them down to the site of Wolf House, which was still under construction. Pointing into the manzanita-scented darkness, he would describe in vivid detail the enormous stone fireplaces; the reflection pool; the redwood balconies; the lofty carriage entrance; the modern refrigeration plant; the roof that was to be done entirely in Spanish tile; the dining room that would seat 50. The cost of Wolf House would run close to $70,000, and when it was finished, London told them, it would be the most beautiful home in California. No one doubted his word. After all, he was Jack London. It was assumed he could do anything.

By this time, London was in the enviable position of being one of the highest-paid authors in the world. He was also one of the most prolific writers of his day. It was typical, in any given year, for the Macmillan Company to publish at least three of London's books. This impressive output was the result of a rigid writing schedule that London had carefully honed over the years. Each morning, starting work shortly after dawn, he would produce a minimum of 1,000 words, and under no circumstances would he allow himself to put aside an unfinished story. "Invariably I complete every one I start," he said in one interview. "If it's good, I sign it and send it out. If it isn't good, I sign it and send it out."

Unfortunately, much of his writing was now beginning to fall into the latter category. Why, reviewers wondered, should the author of *The Sea-Wolf* and *The Call of the Wild* now be turning out such thin material as *Adventure* and *Smoke Bellew* (1912)? As London himself admitted, his reasons for writing had become largely commercial. In addition to supporting his ex-wife, his daughters, his mother, and his stepsister Eliza, London was spending a tremendous amount of money improving his ranch. Until he could turn a profit from the land, there was simply no other way to pay the bills.

"I dream of beautiful horses and fine soil," he told an interviewer at this time. "I dream of the beautiful things I own up in Sonoma County. And I write for no other purpose . . . than to add three or four hundred acres to my

London feeds three of his prize duroc hogs at the Pig Palace. Despite adopting scientific farming techniques, London never succeeded in making the Beauty Ranch pay for itself.

London discusses agriculture with his friend George Wharton James. Although he became increasingly aware that the Beauty Ranch would not fulfill his aspirations, London remained genuinely proud of it.

magnificent estate. . . . To me, my cattle are far more interesting than my profession."

This does not mean, however, that London devoted himself entirely to hackwork. As an artist, he was anxious to maintain his hard-earned reputation, and once or twice a year he would make a point of proving to himself and to the world that he was still capable of producing work of startling originality.

In *Burning Daylight* (1910), London created one of his most popular characters, the swaggering, nearly mythic Elam Harnish, a Yukon hero who makes his fortune during the frenzied gold rush of 1897–98 ("the gosh-dangdest stampede that ever was," Harnish marvels). The novel was a great best-seller in its day, the critics praising its "glowing, vivid style" while simultaneously breathing a sigh of relief that London had "passed through the sad phase of unrest out of which *Martin Eden* grew." Another novel, *The Valley of the Moon* (1913), also sold extremely well.

Certainly, the most successful of London's books from this period was the semi-autobiographical *John Barleycorn*, which created a sensation when it was published in August 1913. Later subtitled "Alcoholic Memoirs," the book was written to illustrate the physical and psychological dangers of hard liquor and to lend encouragement to the growing movement for its prohibition. Unusually perceptive, *John Barleycorn* is a classic in the field of temperance writing, the most personal and most agonizing of all of London's books.

Perhaps too personal. For years, readers (and biographers) have assumed that *John Barleycorn* is completely autobiographical, which it is not. To be sure, there are autobiographical elements—the voyage on the *Sophia Sutherland*, oyster pirating—but, on the whole, it is a fictional story of one man's struggle with alcohol. The "hero" of *John Barleycorn* should not be confused with Jack London himself.

Returning to that distant afternoon when, as a boy, he took his first sip from his stepfather's beer pail, London examines, step-by-step, drink by drink, his protagonist's long association with "the enemy of life," John Barleycorn (a nickname for alcohol). The book is at times repetitive and melodramatic, but, like a doomsday sermon, its heightened sense of urgency cannot be ignored. For the better part of 300 pages, London relentlessly exposes every sordid detail of chemical dependency—the shame, the denial, the hangovers, the fear, the aching, lonely moments when suicide seems a bittersweet temptation.

Never before had an American author dealt so thoroughly, so bluntly, with the subject of alcohol, and *John Barleycorn* became an indispensable weapon in the fight for prohibition. Within a few months of its publication, the book was turned into a popular six-reel film, and over the decades *John Barleycorn* has been translated into more

To raise money to support his family and the ranch, London endorsed a number of products, ranging from suits to grape juice. In this 1913 advertisement, London touts the services of the Royal Tailors.

than 20 languages. It has never gone out of print and is still endorsed by Alcoholics Anonymous.

A few weeks before the publication of *John Barleycorn*, in July 1913, London was stricken with an attack of appendicitis. He was rushed to Merritt Hospital in Oakland, and after the operation, London was told by the surgeon that his kidneys were in terrible condition—so far gone, in fact, that he had only a few years left to live. Although London had often been ill in the past, this news must have come as a terrible shock. His doctor strongly advised him to go on a bland diet and to stop drinking; any amount of alcohol, he was told, could be fatal.

London's period of recuperation was unusually brief. Nine days after his operation, he left Merritt Hospital to stay at his mother's home in Oakland. The newspapers were astonished: "London's recovery is one of the most remarkable in the history of appendicitis operations in this city. . . . He was prevented from going to a prize fight Thursday evening only by the fact that the house was sold out, and since leaving the hospital has been to the theater every evening with Mrs. London, who is his constant companion."

Jack was still recovering from his abdominal operation when, in late August, he and Charmian suffered a devastating loss. The magnificent 26-room Wolf House was in the final stages of construction and, according to the foreman, would soon be ready for occupancy. The heavy stone and timber structure was thought to be fireproof; on the night of August 22, however, Wolf House suddenly, and mysteriously, burned to the ground. Because the house was located in a remote hollow, more than an hour passed before anyone spotted the smoke. By the time London reached the site, it was too late—every room was ablaze. There was no water with which to fight the fire, and he could do nothing but watch as the heavy tile roof collapsed in a spectacular shower of sparks.

Over the years, various stories have circulated about the cause of the inferno. The building superintendent, a stonemason named Forni, believed that an oily rag had spontaneously ignited in the dry August heat, and the existing evidence seems to support this theory. London, on the other hand, was convinced it was a case of arson—the work of a radical, someone who might have considered a 26-room "castle" too grand for a self-proclaimed socialist. Nothing could be proved, however, and, much to the Londons' grief, Wolf House was never rebuilt.

London surveys blueprints during the construction of the 26-room Wolf House . On August 22, 1913, a fire of unknown origin destroyed the nearly completed mansion. Jack and Charmain were emotionally devastated by the loss.

*Jack, Charmian, and Possum pause during a jaunt on the ranch
in 1916. Suffering from the effects of uremia and other afflictions,
London's health declined abruptly toward the end of his life.*

8

Last Battles

SHORTLY AFTER THE FIRE, Jack wrote a caustic letter to his young daughter Joan, who was then living with her mother, Bess, in Oakland. To Jack's disappointment, he had never had a satisfactory relationship with either of his daughters, and the tone of the letter is stingingly blunt, devoid of any familial sentiment:

> What do you feel for me? Am I a fool who gives much and receives nothing? . . . My home—one of my dreams—is destroyed. You have no word to say. . . . Joan, my daughter, please know that the world . . . does not belong to the ones who remain silent, who, by their very silence lie and cheat and make a mock of love and a meal-ticket of their father. Don't you think it is about time I heard from you? Or do you want me to cease forever from caring to hear from you?

It was a harsh letter to write to a 12-year-old, but, at the moment, London was feeling frustrated and unhappy. Still, a reconciliation might have been arranged had it not been for Bess, who seemed to take pleasure in making things difficult for her ex-husband. As a way of

Artist Xavier Martinez, one of London's friends, sketched this cartoon of a bubble blowing contest at the Beauty Ranch. A boisterous, fun-loving man, London reveled in lively conversations and playful high jinks at dinner parties, picnics, and other social gatherings throughout his life.

punishing him for breaking up the family, she refused to let Joan and Becky visit their father at Glen Ellen. Jack, fed up with such pettiness, had retaliated in 1911 by writing a new will, leaving the bulk of the estate to Charmian. Now, in his bitterness, Jack made it clear that he wished to have no further contact with Joan: "Unless I should accidentally meet you on the street, I doubt if I shall ever see you again." (London, however, was unable to permanently turn his back on his eldest daughter. He continued to write to her, but, sadly, Joan had been trained by her mother to distrust her celebrated father. It was a miserable situation for everyone involved.)

The estate from which London had disinherited the girls was by this time one of the largest in Sonoma County. For several years, London had been using his royalties to buy up as much land as possible, and by 1914, the Beauty Ranch totaled more than 1,400 acres. Anyone paying a visit during this period must have noticed that London was becoming quite knowledgeable on the subject of farming. As he frequently told his guests, nothing would give him greater pleasure than to become a full-time rancher, a dawn-to-dusk farmer living off the bounty of the land. "I have pledged myself, my manhood, my fortune, my books, and all I possess to this undertaking."

In his determination to succeed, London subscribed to countless agricultural journals, consulted with experts at the University of California, and read every government bulletin he could lay his hands on. In his own words, he wanted to leave the land better than he had found it; he wanted to grow two blades of grass where only one had grown before. "I am working for results," he wrote proudly, "and I am going to get results that will take their place in books."

His farming methods were considered extremely modern. Everything at the Beauty Ranch was pushed to its potential—London wanted the plumpest chickens, the tastiest carrots, and the healthiest alfalfa and oats. He went out of his way to buy pedigreed pigs and prizewinning bulls; on one occasion, he spent $2,500 for a single shire stallion. A practical farmer, he built the first concrete-block silo in the state of California. His "Pig Palace," as it came to be known, was the most sophisticated in the country, housing up to 250 pampered duroc hogs. (To protect the pigs from disease, London had his visitors sterilize their feet before entering.)

All of these improvements required a great deal of money, and London was spending far more than he was earning. The fire had left him deeply in debt, and bill collectors were constantly harassing him; the threat of being taken to court was a never-ending source of anxiety. One of his longest and most frustrating battles was with the motion picture industry, which was in the process of filming several of his novels without his permission. As London discovered, the copyright laws were poorly written and did little to protect him as an author. At his own expense, he traveled to New York and Hollywood, and, with the help of other writers, managed to convince Congress to pass new legislation giving individual authors greater control over their material. Unfortunately, London did not live long enough to benefit from the new copyright laws. He received only a tiny share of the profits from such films as *John Barleycorn*, *The Sea-Wolf*, and *The Valley of the Moon*.

In April 1914, *Collier's* magazine offered him $1,100 a week plus expenses to go to Mexico and file reports on the Villa-Carranza revolution. It seemed an ideal assignment, but by the time the Londons arrived in the crowded port city of Veracruz, the fighting was drawing to a close. In an attempt to gather information, London went aboard several U.S. Navy ships docked in the harbor, where he interviewed various military personnel. The seven articles that he later submitted to *Collier's* revealed a clearer understanding of the revolution than London has been given credit for. Admittedly, his stance was controversial. To everyone's astonishment, he failed to side with the rebels—"stupid anarchs!" he called them—asserting that as "half-breeds" they were incapable of government rule.

When the first of these articles began appearing, they infuriated members of the Socialist party, who viewed the revolutionaries as working-class heroes rightfully overthrowing a corrupt dictatorship. An impasse between London and the Socialists had been developing for some time, and two years later, in March 1916, London officially resigned from the party of his youth. He had dedicated a great portion of his life to the Socialist cause, and it angered him that the workers had never risen up against "the system," had never tried to wrest the power that could be theirs. He saw no point in continuing his involvement with the party, and his letter of resignation was accepted without comment.

London returned from Mexico in poor health. In Veracruz, he had come down with a serious case of amoebic dysentery, which was followed by pleurisy, an inflammation of the lungs. He was also bothered by a painful swelling in his legs, which may have been rheumatism.

During his long convalescence, London worried continually about his finances. To pay the bills, he turned out a steady stream of novels and short stories, many of which have been forgotten except by a handful of Jack London scholars. The only important novel he wrote during the final two years of his life was *The Star Rover*, a complex and fascinating story of reincarnation based on the real-life experiences of Ed Morrell, a prisoner at nearby San Quentin. Perhaps because of its esoteric subject matter, *The Star Rover* was overlooked when it was published in 1915; only today is it beginning to receive the attention it deserves.

According to Joan London, her father "made no further effort to write well" after finishing *The Star Rover*. This, however, is not a fair assessment; London's imagination was still vigorous and his output was as prolific as ever. Between 1914 and 1916, London completed a minimum of three books a year. For several reasons, though, he was always on the verge of financial ruin. London sensed, correctly, that the public was losing interest in his work. Sales were down, and with the outbreak of World War I in 1914, the European book market dried up completely.

It was also common knowledge that during this period London was extremely generous with his money. Every month, he and Charmian would receive hundreds of letters and telegrams, many of them requests for charitable contributions. Writers, widows, inventors, farmers, convicts, socialists—anyone, it seemed, who was down on their luck—would write a letter to Jack London and, more often than not, receive some sort of financial assistance. (A few of the requests were downright bizarre: Patients suffering from tuberculosis inquired if they could come to the Beauty Ranch to die; a number of frustrated artists wanted London to support their families while they pursued their calling.)

Needless to say, many people took unfair advantage of London's generosity because they felt he could afford it. The greatest part of his yearly income, though, was consumed not by the greedy but by the ranch at Glen Ellen. No matter how hard he worked, no matter how many novels he wrote, London could not make the 1,400-acre estate pay for itself. The soil, exhausted by generations of misuse, was slow to respond to scientific treatment. In 1913, drought set in, scorching the crops; what the winds could not destroy, a swarm of locusts did. The large-scale planting of eucalyptus trees proved to be unprofitable, and during the last weeks of his life, London found himself entangled in a fierce legal battle with his neighbors over water rights. Perhaps the most devastating loss occurred in October 1916, when London's magnificent shire stallion, Neuadd Hillside, was found dead in the pasture. Jack had been exceptionally fond of the horse, and according to Charmian, he wept uncontrollably when he heard the news.

The Roamer *was London's favorite boat during his last years. "Once a sailor, always a sailor," he said of himself. "The savor of the salt never stales."*

These were isolated incidents, however. The ranch was by no means a failure, and Jack and Charmian derived a great deal of pleasure from it. Had London lived longer, he might well have discovered the right mix of crops and livestock that would have allowed the Beauty Ranch to become self-supporting. Unfortunately, time was not on his side: London was slowly dying of uremia. As his kidneys gradually lost their ability to function, waste products began to accumulate in his bloodstream; this, in turn, allowed toxins to spread throughout his body. It was a painful and frightening disease, with many unpleasant side effects. Today, dialysis machines regularly assist failing kidneys, but in the years preceding World War I there was almost no hope for recovery.

In an effort to regain his health, London made two extended trips to the Hawaiian Islands in 1915 and 1916. These were delightful vacations. In nearly every photo, London looks relaxed and happy. He no longer had the energy for surfboarding; instead, he and Charmian spent their time reading books, walking along the beach, attend-

In 1915, Jack and Charmian pose on a hammock in a photographer's studio in Honolulu. In an effort to help Jack recuperate from his various ailments, the Londons vacationed in the Hawaiian Islands in 1915 and 1916.

ing horse races, and reacquainting themselves with old friends. They revisited the leper colony at Molokai, and, on New Year's Eve, 1915, they were invited to a distinguished reception for Queen Liliuokalani, deposed ruler of the Hawaiian Islands.

During both trips, London remained in fine spirits. He was a bit paunchy around the middle, but, then again, so was Charmian—teasingly, he called her Fatty. London participated in as many group activities as he could, and because of this, none of the islanders suspected that he was ill. London's uremia was a well-kept secret.

He and Charmian returned to the Beauty Ranch in July 1916. The period that followed marked a steady decline in London's health. "I've never been quite right since my sickness and operation in Australia," he told Charmian confidentially. "But don't worry, don't bother, I'll be all right, my dear."

By this time, London's doctor had taught him how to use a hypodermic syringe, and whenever the pain became intolerable, London was able to find relief in morphine, a powerful anesthetic that provided hours of much-needed sleep. He may also have injected himself with opium, which at that time was a legal drug. A few of London's biographers have written that, during this period, London drank heavily to deaden the pain. According to author Upton Sinclair, London could be seen "wandering about the bars of Oakland, dazed and disagreeably drunk." This is highly unlikely: London was consuming very little alcohol at the time, and he was never seen in public in an intoxicated state. Accounts of his adult drinking have been wildly exaggerated.

As London's health worsened, Charmian did everything she could to assist him. She, too, learned to handle the hypodermic, and during the last weeks of her husband's life, she was at his bedside frequently, massaging his swollen ankles, wiping the sweat from his brow—ready, if necessary, to inject the needle to ease his suffering.

A groom exercises Neuadd Hillside, London's favorite shire stallion. Jack was exceptionally fond of the horse and wept uncontrollably when he was informed of its sudden death.

On Tuesday, November 21, 1916, London did not feel well and spent most of the day dozing. That evening, over a dinner of wild duck, he and his stepsister Eliza discussed ways in which the ranch might be turned into a farming commune. Then, complaining of fatigue, London took two trays of reading material and retired to his room for the night.

It was still early, and, feeling restless, Charmian decided to go for a walk. Upon returning an hour later, she noticed that London's reading light was still on. Glancing in, she saw him propped up in bed, his eyes closed, his chin resting comfortably on his chest. It was not often that Jack was able to enjoy a good night's sleep, and Charmian dared not disturb him. She quietly returned to her own room and, exhausted by the last few days, fell into a deep slumber.

The next morning, shortly before 8 o'clock, the Japanese servant went to awaken London, as he did every morning. A moment later, Sekine came flying out of the room, panicked, calling for help. Charmian threw on a wrapper and hurried to her husband's room, where others had already gathered. One look told her that London was gravely ill: His face was dark blue, and his breathing was heavy. Someone ran for the telephone, but it was out of order. London's secretary immediately went to fetch medical help. London, meanwhile, did not seem to be conscious of anything that was happening around him.

Dr. Allan Thomson, a physician from Sonoma, arrived at the ranch at approximately 8:30 A.M. By this time, London was in a coma. Glancing around, Thomson spotted a nearly-empty morphine vial on the floor. Logically, he assumed that London had injected himself with an overdose of morphine. Phone service to the ranch, meanwhile, had been restored, and Thomson immediately telephoned his assistant, Dr. Hayes, and asked him to bring a stomach pump and an antidote for morphine poisoning.

At noon, a third physician arrived from San Francisco. Shortly thereafter, London's personal doctor, William Porter, arrived from Oakland. Dr. Porter was aware, as the others were not, that his patient was suffering from terminal uremia. He quickly told his colleagues that London's failing kidneys had allowed toxins to build up in his bloodstream. The accumulation of poisons, Porter explained, was responsible for the coma. The morphine overdose—if, indeed, London had taken one—was incidental.

The physicians worked feverishly to revive their patient. Every type of stimulant was administered—hot coffee, a stomach pump, limb massage, and vigorous shaking. It was vital, the doctors said, to keep London's heart pumping. He was hauled to his feet and walked back and forth across the room. Someone even yelled that the newly completed dam had burst, hoping to get a startled reaction. At this moment, according to Charmian, her husband slowly began "beating the mattress with a loosely-clenched right fist. The left was never raised." This has led at least one biographer, Russ Kingman, to suspect that London may have suffered a paralytic stroke.

Late in the afternoon, London was carried onto his wife's sleeping porch, where he died at approximately 7:45 that evening, November 22, 1916. He was 40 years old. A press bulletin was immediately released, citing the cause of death as "a gastro-intestinal type of uremia."

Two days later, London's body was taken to Oakland to be cremated. Before the casket was closed, however, his

Sculptor Finn Frolich puts the finishing touches on his bust of Jack London. "I never saw a man in all my life with more magnetism . . . ," Frolich remembered.

On November 26, 1916, London's cremated remains were buried on the Beauty Ranch. A large boulder of volcanic rock, rejected by the builders of Wolf House, was rolled over his grave. The grave site and the charred ruins of Wolf House are now part of the Jack London State Historical Park in Glen Ellen.

servant Sekine slipped a loving message into the breast pocket of London's jacket. "Your Speech was silver," it read, "now your Silence is golden."

On Sunday, November 26, London's ashes were laid to rest at the Beauty Ranch. After the simple ceremony, an enormous red boulder was placed over his grave. Today, the grave site and the charred ruins of Wolf House are visited by thousands of people each year at the Jack London State Historical Park in Glen Ellen.

.   .   .

In the early years of the 20th century, Jack London helped to introduce a new and gritty realism into American literature. It is partly for this reason that his novels and short stories continue to enjoy worldwide popularity. *The Call of the Wild* and *Martin Eden*, in particular, have lost none of their bristling vitality. They remain important works of American fiction.

At the same time, there is another dimension to Jack London that continues to fascinate the public—his highly dramatic personal life. He was one of the great adventurers of his day. It is with excitement and a keen sense of longing that we read of his exploits in the Far North; of his remarkable two-year voyage on the *Snark*; of his ambitious, and heartbreaking, attempt to build the most beautiful home in the state of California. Like the hero in his novel *Burning Daylight*, London was a high-stakes gambler, intoxicated by the game of life. "I would rather be ashes than dust!" he once wrote, summing up in a few words his rich and vigorous philosophy:

> I would rather be a superb meteor, every atom of me in magnificent glow, than a sleepy and permanent planet. The proper function of man is to live, not to exist.
>
> I shall not waste my days in trying to prolong them.
>
> I shall use my time.

Appendix

Books By Jack London

This chronological list provides the years of publication and original publishers of all of Jack London's books. Some titles are currently out-of-print or available from publishers other than the ones listed.

The Son of the Wolf. New York: Houghton Mifflin & Co., 1900. Short stories. Published in Britain as *An Odyssey of the North.*

The God of His Fathers. New York: McClure, Phillips & Co., 1901. Short stories.

The Children of the Frost. New York: The Macmillan Co., 1902. Short stories.

The Cruise of the Dazzler. New York: The Century Co., 1902. Juvenile novel.

A Daughter of the Snows. Philadelphia: J. B. Lippincott Co., 1902. Novel.

The Kempton-Wace Letters. New York: The Macmillan Co., 1903. Epistolary novel, coauthored by Jack London and Anna Strunsky.

The Call of the Wild. New York: The Macmillan Co., 1903. Novel.

The People of the Abyss. New York: The Macmillan Co., 1903. Sociological study of London's slum conditions.

The Faith of Men. New York: The Macmillan Co., 1904. Short stories.

The Sea-Wolf. New York: The Macmillan Co., 1904. Novel.

The War of the Classes. New York: The Macmillan Co., 1905. Sociological essays.

The Game. New York: The Macmillan Co., 1905. Novel.

Tales of the Fish Patrol. New York: The Macmillan Co., 1905. Juvenile short stories.

Moon-Face and Other Stories. New York: The Macmillan Co., 1906. Short stories.

White Fang. New York: The Macmillan Co., 1906. Novel.

Scorn of Women. New York: The Macmillan Co., 1906. Play.

Before Adam. New York: The Macmillan Co., 1907. Novel.

Love of Life and Other Stories. New York: The Macmillan Co., 1907. Short stories.

The Road. New York: The Macmillan Co., 1907. Essays.

The Iron Heel. New York: The Macmillan Co., 1908. Novel.

Martin Eden. New York: The Macmillan Co., 1909. Novel.

Lost Face. New York: The Macmillan Co., 1910. Short stories.

Revolution and Other Essays. New York: The Macmillan Co., 1910. Essays.

Burning Daylight. New York: The Macmillan Co., 1910. Novel.

Theft. New York: The Macmillan Co., 1910. Play.

When God Laughs and Other Stories. New York: The Macmillan Co., 1911. Short stories.

Adventure. New York: The Macmillan Co., 1911. Novel.

The Cruise of the Snark. New York: The Macmillan Co., 1911. Collected travel articles.

South Sea Tales. New York: The Macmillan Co., 1911. Short stories.

The House of Pride. New York: The Macmillan Co., 1912. Short stories.

A Son of the Sun. New York: Doubleday, Page & Co., 1912. Short stories.

Smoke Bellew. New York: The Century Co., 1912. Connected short stories. Published in Britain in two volumes, *Smoke Bellew* and *Smoke and Shorty*.

The Night Born. New York: The Century Co., 1913. Short stories.

The Abysmal Brute. New York: The Century Co., 1913. Novel.

John Barleycorn. New York: The Century Co., 1913. Sociological study of the effects of alcohol.

The Valley of the Moon. New York: The Macmillan Co., 1913. Novel.

The Strength of the Strong. New York: The Macmillan Co., 1914. Short stories.

The Mutiny of the Elsinore. New York: The Macmillan Co., 1914. Novel. Serialized under the title "The Sea Gangsters."

The Scarlet Plague. New York: The Macmillan Co., 1915. Novel.

The Star Rover. New York: The Macmillan Co., 1915. Novel. Published in Britain as *The Jacket*.

The Acorn Planter. New York: The Macmillan Co., 1916. Play.

The Little Lady of the Big House. New York: The Macmillan Co., 1916. Novel.

The Turtles of Tasman. New York: The Macmillan Co., 1916. Short stories. Last book published during London's lifetime.

The Human Drift. New York: The Macmillan Co., 1917. Essays.

Jerry of the Islands. New York: The Macmillan Co., 1917. Novel.

Michael, Brother of Jerry. New York: The Macmillan Co., 1917. Novel.

The Red One. New York: The Macmillan Co., 1918. Short stories.

On the Makaloa Mat. New York: The Macmillan Co., 1919. Short stories.

Hearts of Three. New York: The Macmillan Co., 1920. Novel.

Dutch Courage and Other Stories. New York: The Macmillan Co., 1922. Short stories.

The Assassination Bureau, Ltd. New York: McGraw-Hill Book Co., 1963. Novel. Half-finished at the time of London's death, the book was completed by Robert L. Fish.

Chronology

Jan. 12, 1876	Born in San Francisco, California
Sept. 1876	Flora Wellman marries John London
1891	Buys *Razzle Dazzle*, becomes oyster pirate
1893	Joins crew of sealing schooner *Sophia Sutherland*; returns to Oakland, August 26
1894	Joins the Industrial Army; becomes hobo, is incarcerated in Erie County Penitentiary
1897–1898	London seeks his fortune in the Klondike; death of stepfather, John, October 15, 1897
Jan. 1899	Publication of short story "To the Man on Trail" in *Overland Monthly*
April 7, 1900	Publication of first book, *The Son of the Wolf*, and marriage to Bess Maddern
1902	Trip to London, England, to investigate slum conditions
1903	Publication of *The Call of the Wild* and *The People of the Abyss*; abandons family
1904	Goes to Japan to cover the Russo-Japanese War; publication of *The Sea-Wolf*
Nov. 19, 1905	Marries Charmian Kittredge
1907–1909	Voyage of the *Snark*; Jack and Charmian return to Glen Ellen, July 1909
1908	Publication of *The Iron Heel*
1909	Publication of *Martin Eden*
1913	Publication of *John Barleycorn*; burning of Wolf House, August 22
1915	Publication of last important book, *The Star Rover*; five-month trip to Hawaiian Islands
Nov. 22, 1916	Death in Glen Ellen, California

Further Reading

Barltrop, Robert. *Jack London: The Man, the Writer, the Rebel.* London: Pluto Press, 1976.

Hedrick, Joan D. *Solitary Comrade: Jack London and His Work.* Chapel Hill: University of North Carolina Press, 1982.

Hendricks, King, and Irving Shepard, eds. *Jack London Reports.* New York: Doubleday, 1970.

———. *Letters from Jack London.* New York: Odyssey Press, 1965.

Kingman, Russ. *A Pictorial Life of Jack London.* New York: Crown, 1979.

London, Charmian. *The Book of Jack London.* 2 vols. New York: Century, 1921.

———. *The Log of the Snark.* New York: Macmillan, 1915.

London, Jack. *The Cruise of the Snark.* New York: Macmillan, 1911.

———. *John Barleycorn.* New York: Century, 1913; Santa Cruz, CA: Western Tanager Press, 1981.

London, Joan. *Jack London and His Times.* Garden City, NY: Doubleday, 1939.

O'Connor, Richard. *Jack London: A Biography.* Boston: Little, Brown, 1964.

Sinclair, Andrew. *Jack: A Biography of Jack London.* New York: HarperCollins, 1977.

Stasz, Clarice. *American Dreamers: Charmian and Jack London.* New York: St. Martin's Press, 1988.

Stone, Irving. *Sailor on Horseback.* Cambridge, MA: Houghton Mifflin, 1938.

Walker, Franklin. *Jack London and the Klondike.* San Marino, CA: Huntington Library, 1972.

Index

PICTURE CREDITS

The Bettmann Archive: frontispiece, pp. 10, 25, 28, 39, 40, 43, 47, 48, 50, 55, 60, 61, 64, 68, 85, 91, 92; Department of Parks and Recreation, Santa Rosa, CA: pp. 14 (#175-16), 16 (#126.2), 18 (#40.0ql), 31 (#26.9), 32 (#42.14ql), 73, 82 (#36.24ql), 93 (#349.6), 96 (#117.1), 99 (#23.29), 102, 106 (#113.2), 109, 110, 115 (#14.13), 116 (#36.10ql), 117 (#18.11), 119 (#58.12), 120 (#40.12); Huntington Library Collection and Botanical Gardens: pp. 70, 74, 95; Courtesy of Russ Kingman, with permission of the Jack London Estate: pp. 20, 21, 22, 36, 59, 63, 67, 75, 76, 79, 81, 88, 100, 105, 108, 112; Maps by Gary Tong: pp. 13, 53

ACKNOWLEDGMENTS

The author dedicates this book to Mabel H. Morris, who cared for Jack London when she was a student nurse at Merritt Hospital in Oakland, California.
Many thanks also to Russ Kingman for his invaluable comments.

Alan Schroeder is the author of *Josephine Baker* (1991) written for the Chelsea House series BLACK AMERICANS OF ACHIEVEMENT. He is also the author of *Ragtime Tumpie* (1989), a fictionalized account of Josephine Baker's childhood in St. Louis. *Ragtime Tumpie* was selected by several magazines as one of the best children's books of 1989. It was also named a Notable Children's Book of 1989 by the American Library Association. Mr. Schroeder lives in Alameda, California.

Vito Perrone is Director of Teacher Education and Chair of Teaching, Curriculum, and Learning Environments at Harvard University. He has previous experience as a public school teacher, a university professor of history, education, and peace studies (University of North Dakota), and as dean of the New School and Center for Teaching and Learning (both at the University of North Dakota). Dr. Perrone has written extensively about such issues as educational equity, humanities curriculum, progress in education, and evaluation. His most recent books are: *A Letter to Teachers: Reflections on Schooling and the Art of Teaching; Enlarging Student Assessment in Schools; Working Papers: Reflections on Teachers, Schools, and Communities; Visions of Peace;* and *Johanna Knudsen Miller: A North Dakota Pioneer Teacher.*